STITCH, FABRIC & THREAD

Dedication
To Patrick, my husband
and best friend.

Acknowledgements

First, I would like to thank Katie French for giving me the opportunity to write this book. I'd like to thank … … and shows what can h… … someone with a book i… … her enthusiasm, imagina… … hotography, and Juar… … ook so good.

Than… … or allowing me

On a… … ibuting to the 'Fluxus … … ut most of all for way… … d friend.

Finally, … … or his willingness to offer himself as a sounding board for my ideas.

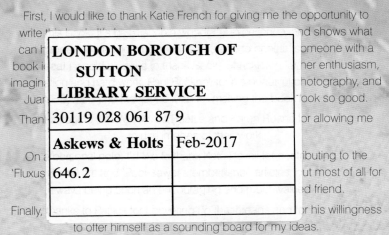
First published in 2017

Search Press Limited
Wellwood, North Farm Road,
Tunbridge Wells, Kent TN2 3DR

Text copyright © Elizabeth Healey 2017

Photographic credits: 23 © neftali / Shutterstock.com;
24l, 24c, 25, 96, 123bl, 123bc, 123br, 126l, 126tr, 136tl ©
Elizabeth Healey; 43t © ullstein bild / Getty; 43b © Paromita
Banerjee; 48 © Extra Special Touch personalised men's
cotton hemstitch handkerchief / Heidi Lawton; 49t © Extra
Special Touch classic monogram linen napkin / Mirror Imaging
Photography; 49b © Hurst Photo / Shutterstock.com;
54tl © Milton Glaser; 88 © Jim Wilson; 89b © Jo Beattie;
115: thanks to Kate Cross; 125: thanks to Sylvia Critcher;
130 inset © Extra Special Touch Nottingham lace
handkerchief with custom embroidery design /
Randolph Wilcox Photography; 132bl © Karen Ruane;
136bl © Patrick O'Sullivan

All other photographs by Paul Bricknell

Illustrations by Bess Harding

Photographs, illustrations and design copyright
© Search Press Ltd 2017

ISBN: 978-1-78221-285-0

Suppliers
For details of suppliers, please visit the Search Press website:
www.searchpress.com

Printed in China

STITCH, FABRIC & THREAD

AN INSPIRATIONAL GUIDE FOR CREATIVE STITCHERS

Elizabeth Healey

SEARCH PRESS

CONTENTS

INTRODUCTION

I learned to sew not by sitting at my grandmother's knee – I was too young to benefit from her experience before she passed away, although I'm told she was a skilled needlewoman who could turn her expert hand to just about any craft from lace making and knitting to sewing. Instead, my interest in fabric and sewing was first piqued on an airfield, of all places, while I watched my Dad restore an Auster MK 5: an aircraft used by the military for observation purposes during WWII.

I was fascinated by how a needle and thread could help make a plane fly! Admittedly, the thick sheets of Irish linen laid over the plane's framework were the size of pillowcases; the needles that sewed them together were as long as my arm, with thread the thickness and strength of butcher's twine – but it was still sewing.

This childhood memory explains two things: firstly my love of linen, and secondly why I often use unusual materials in my sewing projects. It taught me that sewing doesn't have to be just about buying and following patterns, it can also be about play, improvisation and doing the unexpected – qualities I hope you will find in this book.

It is one thing to be told 'go ahead, be creative, just play and see what happens', but quite another to produce something coherent that you are actually happy with. A blank sheet of paper can be a daunting sight for even the most confident designer, especially if they are expected to fill it with original and well-planned designs – often to a tight deadline. In such situations, designers rely on training that equips them with a range of skills and techniques they can draw on to help turn a vague idea into a fully realised design. A few of these skills are included in this book:

- Working up ideas through sketchbooks and swatches in order to develop ideas and smooth out rough edges before committing to a final design
- Using colour
- Deciding on a composition
- Using type
- Creating patterns using reference material
- Choosing tools and materials that best suit the job.

Any designer worth their salt will also know the value of looking beyond the obvious for inspiration, and this is something else I try to encourage you to do. Although this book is split into several basic sections – things to consider before you start sewing, commonly used stitches and how you can further embellish and manipulate fabric – I suggest using unusual sources for inspiration throughout. Sometimes these are contained within the projects themselves, at other times they are suggested in feature spreads called Behind the Stitches, which shine a light on influential textiles and the people who made them. Many of these makers are ordinary people who make (or made) extraordinary yet functional textiles. They do not rely on expensive gadgets and fashionable fabric ranges in order to sew. Instead, they use what comes to hand to produce beautiful textiles that tell of personal stories and generations speaking to one another through the language of cloth, needle and thread. Improvisation is often at the core of the making, and the stories, motifs, colours and patterns depicted vary according to the maker's personal interpretation of a theme.

In much the same way that many of the makers I've used as inspiration do not strictly follow a set pattern, the point of this book isn't to show you how to perfectly replicate every sample included in its pages. Although some steps, tips and techniques are provided, and some templates included at the back of the book (in case you do want to try your hand at a particular project), the aim is to nudge you in a direction from which your own ideas develop. With a needle and thread and a little imagination anything is possible: who knows, you might even make a plane fly.

"Inspiration does exist, but it must find you working." – Pablo Picasso

"The hand is the tool of tools." – Aristotle

BEFORE THE STITCHES

Preparation is key to the success of a project. Doing your research and knowing which tools and materials to use will help avoid disappointment and result in work of which you can be proud.

TOOLS: EVERYTHING OR NOTHING

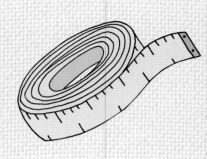

When it comes to tools, stitchers tend to fall into one of two categories: those who need everything, or those who make do with very little. Whichever category you fall into, or maybe if you're somewhere in between, always look after your tools.

A basic kit should include the following

Scissors: I recommend you buy the best you can afford and store them in wallets to prevent the tips getting blunted and bashed by other equipment. A pair of fabric shears (1), some general purpose scissors (2), dedicated paper scissors (3) and a pair of embroidery scissors (4) are the essentials. NEVER use your fabric or embroidery scissors to cut paper; it's a sure-fire way to blunt them! Other cutting tools that you might find useful include: rotary cutters (5), pinking shears (6), snips and a thread cutter (7), which can be worn as a pendant if you like to sew on the go!

Pins: It's worth having an assortment of pins (8). Silks won't take kindly to having hefty pins shoved through them so you'll need some fine, sharp, straight-head pins for delicate fabrics. If you are working with heavier fabrics, such as tweeds and sturdy felts, I find knitters' and quilters' pins (9) useful. Old-fashioned nappy pins (10) are ideal for holding quilt layers together and look pretty too.

Needles: Likewise, you'll need a range of sewing needles (11) that are suited to the fabrics and materials you work with. If, like me, you often have trouble threading your needle, a needle threader (12) is essential. The ingenious Italian model shown right (which reminds me of an old fashioned steam train) is a godsend!

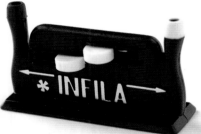

My other essentials include

A **seam ripper** (13: because nobody's perfect), a pair of **tweezers** (14) and a **thimble** (15), I like a coin thimble, as I dislike the total lack of sensation you get with the rigid kind – but see what works best for you. I'd also be lost without my **water-soluble pens** (16), a range of **embroidery hoops** (17: vital for keeping an even tension across your work), a **tape measure** (18) and finally, some **double-pointed knitting needles** (dpns: 19) for poking out corners.

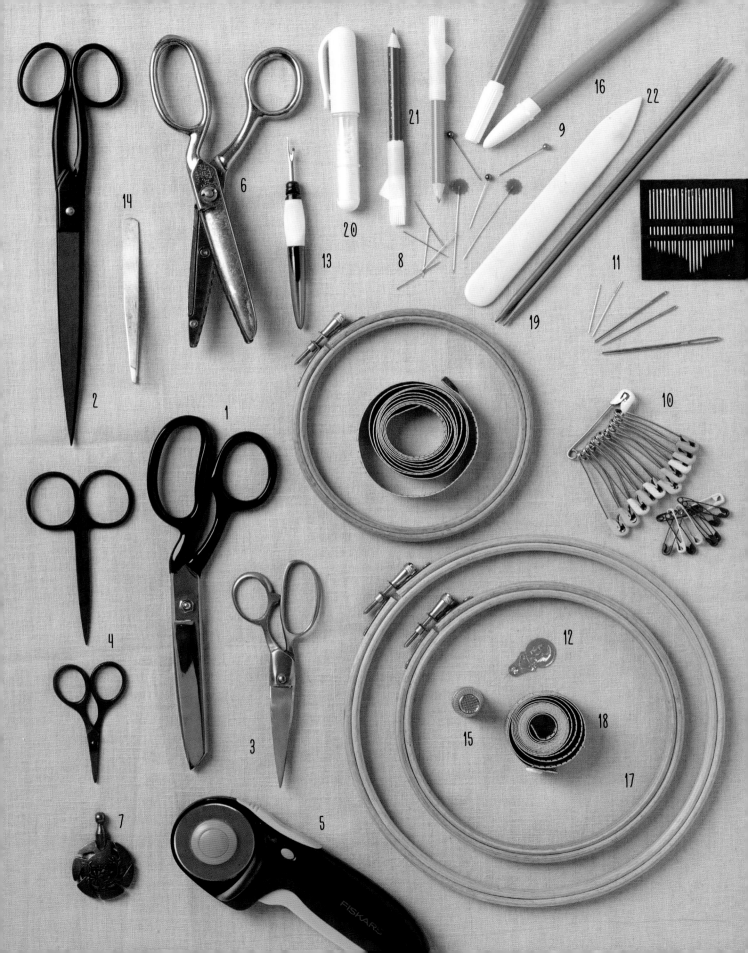

HOW A SEWING MACHINE WORKS

The most expensive piece of kit you're likely to buy will be a sewing machine. The model you choose will depend on personal preference and budget. However, whether you buy one with bells and whistles, or just the necessary basics, the principle of how each works is exactly the same.

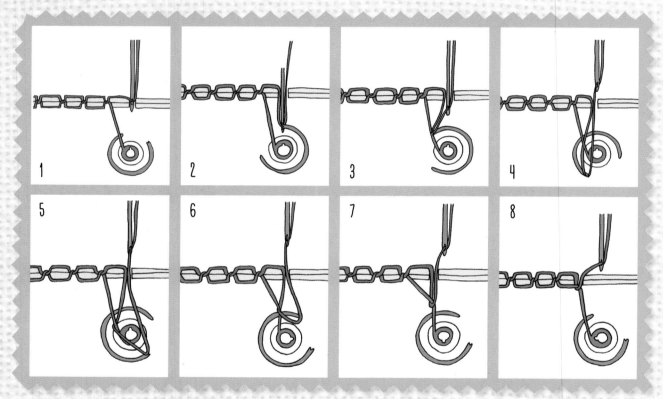

Stitch mechanics

1. The needle pierces the fabric while the hook on the bobbin case rotates anti-clockwise towards the needle.

2. The hook on the bobbin case comes into contact with the needle's thread and catches it…

3. …Pulling it towards the bobbin thread.

4. The threads interlock as the hook continues to rotate, bringing the needle thread around with it.

NB: once the needle is no longer in the fabric, the fabric can move along the feed dogs.

5. The hook releases the thread.

6. As the needle rises to its uppermost position, the bobbin and needle threads are drawn together on the bottom layer of the fabric.

7. The cycle is almost complete. How tightly the stitches bind together will depend on how you set your tension.

8. A stitch has been completed and the process starts all over again.

THE IMPORTANCE OF SKETCHBOOKS

There is great comfort in following a design created by someone else, be it a shop-bought kit, an article in a magazine, a book or even an online tutorial, since much of the planning and thinking is done for you. All you have to do is follow the instructions and you should get a replica of what's on the packet. Coming up with your own design is far more daunting and can be filled with frustrating moments as you strive to realise your vision. But when you get it right, it is infinitely more satisfying than anything bought off the shelf.

The first step to creating your own design is gathering reference and making sense of it. This is why it is so important to keep notebooks rather than just hold everything in your head, or stuck on Pinterest boards (which do of course have their place).Try to get into the habit of always carrying a notebook around with you to jot down your ideas. Don't worry if you can't draw – words and simple mark-making are often enough to remind you of that brilliant but fleeting piece of inspiration that would otherwise have been lost, had it not been recorded.

When you get home, transfer your jottings to larger sketchbooks where you can include little stitch doodles on scraps of fabric, or directly onto the pages, that indicate the direction your design might take. Your sketchbooks are where you can afford to make mistakes so be experimental and try out lots of options before committing them to any precious fabrics.

When you are confident of your idea, continue to use your sketchbook throughout the making of your project. Use it for working out dimensions, and listing what you need, and any adjustments you make during the making process. That way, what you'll end up with is two projects in one: your fully realised design, and the story of how it came to be made.

Q: WHAT IS THREAD?

Good question: well, here are some possibilities... for everyday sewing, **cotton** thread is ideal for delicate fabrics but it does tend to break easily and doesn't have much give. **Polyester** thread is a more durable, all-purpose thread, often with a wax or silicone coating that allows it to glide through fabrics. **Heavy-duty cotton**, as the name suggests, is for more robust fabrics such as those used in upholstery, or denims, canvases and heavy linens. **Silk** thread is extremely fine and doesn't leave holes so is perfect for using on delicate or lingerie-weight fabrics. When it comes to embroidery, **stranded cotton, polyester** and **silk** are amongst the most common; they come in skeins and tend to get into a terrible tangle unless you wind them on to bobbins before use. My personal favourite is **cotton perlé**, which is a twisted glossy thread, that comes in solid and variegated colours, I often substitute this for *sashiko* **cotton** as I find it easier to work with. Other embroidery threads include **soft embroidery cotton, metallic** threads – both real and synthetic – **crewel wool**, which is a fine, 2-ply wool, and **tapestry wool**, which is a tightly twisted 4-ply wool – not dissimilar to knitting wool, which of course can also be used for sewing. But why not go off-piste and try something less conventional? **Jute string** isn't just for tying brown paper packages, it can also be used for sewing, as can **butchers'** or **bakers' rayon twine, labelling cotton, sisal twine, polished flax twine** and **raffia. Ribbons, tightly twisted thin strips of fabric remnants, piping cord, paper string,** jeweller's **leather cord** and even **shoelaces** work perfectly as thread as long as the material they are sewing through has an open enough weave. Rather than visit a haberdashery, see what the chandler has in store – you'll be surprised at what you can find there: **brightly coloured braids** and **elasticated ropes** of varying thickness, sailors' **whipping twine** – ideal for bookbinding – all make fabulous alternatives to traditional threads. Household items such as **dental floss** (yes really!) is surprisingly lovely to sew with, and smells minty fresh too, while **plastic bags shredded into strips** are an excellent source of recycled thread! Tough on the hands, but well worth trying, are materials such as **picture hanging wire, copper fuse wire, beaders' wire** and **fishing wire.** Even a spool of garden wire (the sort you snap off and twist) can be reimagined as thread. If you're friends with a musician, ask if they've got any spare **guitar strings**, or a broken violin bow from which you can strip the **horsehair.** A word of caution on these last few items though: it would be wise to wear protective gloves and goggles when handling them... *and stock up on hand cream... you'll need it!*

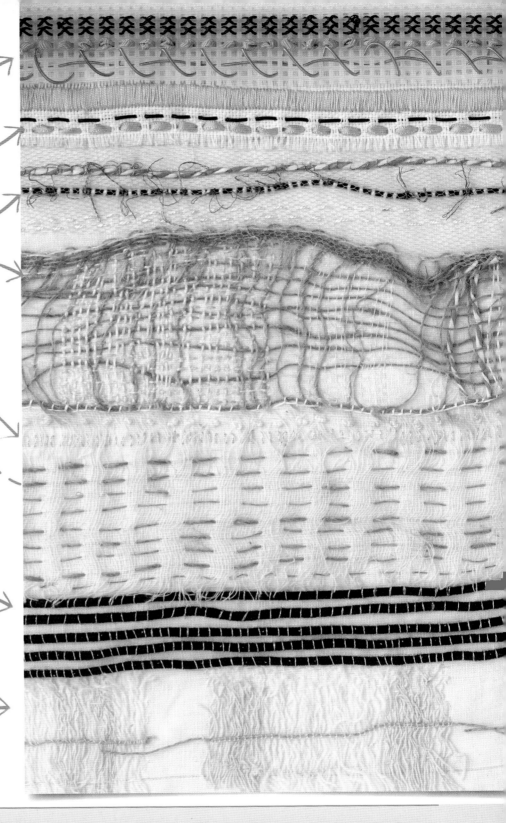

From the top:

Sailors' whipping twine, a thin piece of Petersham ribbon and a guitar string are worked into a strip of plastic embroidery canvas.

Cotton perlé, fine leather jewellery cord and a skinny silk ribbon are woven through Aida cloth.

Paper string, thicker leather cord, curtain cord and copper fuse wire sewn into tutu netting.

Builders' jute embellished with variegated cotton perlé, cotton thread, paper string and dental floss.

Embroidery floss, metallic thread, Sisal and jewellery wire on a scrim background.

Shoe laces couched with silver metallic thread.

Merino yarn, *sashiko* thread and gardening string are unravelled and the tufts held in place with a combination of fine paper string, nylon beading thread and threads pulled from the above scrim.

 The short answer is that virtually anything can be used as thread as long as the material you're sewing into has an open enough weave to accommodate it.

WHAT IS FABRIC?

I have a magpie-like approach to choosing fabrics and often find myself sewing onto backgrounds that weren't originally developed for use in textiles. In the past, I have found dust sheets and dish cloths surprisingly good to sew with, while experimenting with plastic and building mesh has produced results that I'm sure will one day be put to good use.

GET INTO GOOD HABITS

When you start sewing, it's hard to resist the urge to build up a ridiculously large stash of fabric. You find yourself buying fabrics you have no immediate use for, because you worry that stock will run out, or you've simply fallen for the latest, must-have range of designer prints. Inevitably, you'll end up giving many of these impulse buys away (usually to make space for more), which is great for the lucky recipients but not so good for your purse. Instead, try to get into the habit early on of knowing what fabrics you like. This doesn't mean you have to be blinkered, or can't experiment with different fabrics, but be guided by your own taste, not that of fashion, or marketing departments, and buy your cloth accordingly – that way you'll save money.

However, it is worth having a range of fabrics in your collection, since different types of fabric suggest various moods and purposes. Everyone has their own way of organising their fabrics; some do it by colour, others by prints and solids – find what works for you. I divide mine by texture as I find it easier to mix and match that way.

COTTON AND LINEN

These take up by far the biggest proportion of my fabric collection:

1. Solid and printed quilting cottons.

2. Liberty prints.

3. Poplin: a tightly woven cotton, which, like Liberty lawn, is very crisp and perfect for quilting.

4. Linen with a fine thread count: because linen is a natural fibre it holds colour beautifully. It's always my first choice when I want subtle, dusty tones.

5. Very coarse linen: this works well for drawn and pulled thread work, or if you want a noticeable texture in your work.

6. Denims and men's shirts.

7. Cotton organdie.

8. Single colour cottons with a texture woven, or pressed into them.

9. Printed linens.

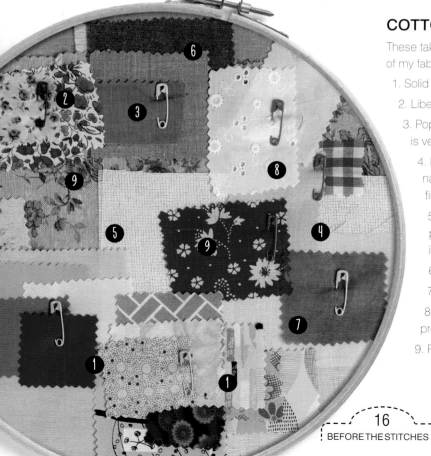

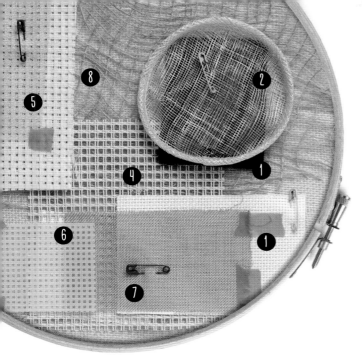

OPEN WEAVE

1. Black and white Aida fabrics: designed for cross stitching and geometric patterns, the warp and weft threads are grouped into bundles. These bundles form a natural mesh which makes it obvious where to insert the needle – especially useful when following charts. I also use Aida cloth for drawn and pulled thread work.

2. Sinamay: this is usually used in millinery as it holds its shape really well.

3. Sacking: can be bought especially for craft and sewing projects. Sacking is usually quite coarse and made from hessian. Old coffee sacks, or feed sacks (if you can get your hands on them) are great to sew into, as hessian ages well.

4. Tapestry canvas.

5. Plastic netting.

6. Plastic embroidery canvas.

7. Copper mesh.

8. Plasterers' jute scrim.

THICKER

1. Japanese woven fabrics: these are often just as interesting on their reverse side.

2. Felt: whether shop-bought, or salvaged from laundry mishaps, felt is a delight to sew into.

3. Tweeds: fabulously warm and earthy, I use these in big blocks for winter quilts.

4. Suiting fabrics: if there's a men's tailor near you, ask if they will sell you a bag of scraps.

5. Flannel: old pyjamas make wonderful backings for quilts. I like to retain features such as pockets and buttonhole plackets.

6. Furnishing fabrics: upholsterers will often sell (or even give away) sample books of discontinued lines of fabrics.

7. Vintage bark cloth.

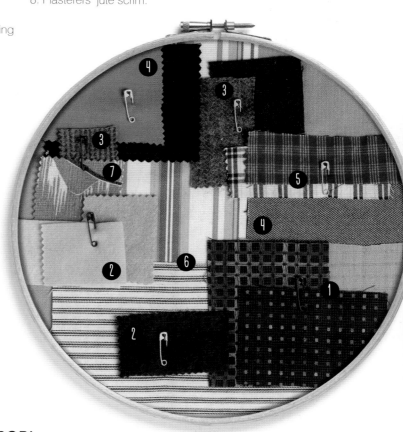

SHIBORI

A collection of all things indigo!

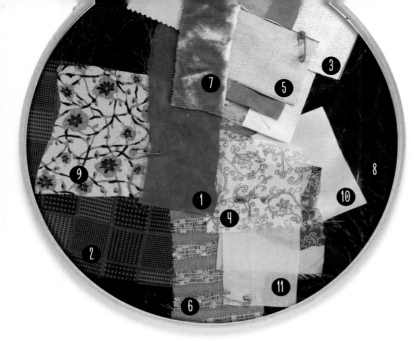

LUXURY

I like to combine slinky fabrics with coarser fabrics for an interesting contrast:

1. Silk: genuine silk always feels cool to the touch.

2. Man-made silk: this might look nearly as good as the real thing, but it won't feel the same.

3. Shot silk taffeta: has a lovely texture and catches the light well.

4. Chiffon: perfect for layering over other fabrics to create a misty effect.

5. Silk dupion.

6. Textured silk.

7. Silk velvet: slippery as oysters to work with but worth the aggravation because of its beauty.

8. Crushed velvet.

9. Silk kimono sleeves.

10. Satin.

11. Silk organza.

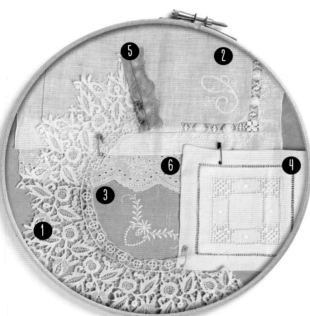

DELICATES

I like to incorporate a lot of vintage fabrics, especially lace and embroidery, into other projects:

1. Detachable lace collars and cuffs: some from my collection date back to the 1920s.

2. Monogrammed hankies.

3. Vintage linen table wear.

4. Embroidered lavender sachets.

5. Lace trim from a vintage nightie.

6. Scraps of *broderie Anglaise*.

SOME RECYCLING TIPS

• Save labels and washing instructions in a notebook so you can refer to them at a later date.

• Before cutting into a garment, locate the grain line and mark it with a water-soluble pen or a piece of masking tape.

• Check for evidence of moths! If there's anything suspicious, or you've bought second hand, place the garment in a plastic bag and freeze for at least twelve hours. Then wash it at as high a temperature as laundry instructions permit.

• Never store just-bought vintage items with other fabrics. Always freeze and wash them first – you don't want any stowaways eating their way through the rest of your stash.

• If a garment smells, wash it! If it still smells after washing, or there are unsightly stains or a network of moth holes, then it's not worth recycling. Make, do and mend is all well and good, but know when to call it a day.

MIXED

This is a bit of a lucky dip as lots of unusual stuff gets thrown in with this collection, which I immediately forget about, so am often surprised whenever I have a rummage:

1. Long-life supermarket plastic bags: these usually have an inbuilt mesh, which means you could transcribe charts onto them.

2. Plastic carrier bags.

3. Builders' mesh.

4. Dusters: lovely and soft, rather like felt.

5. Tea towels.

6. Foam rubber: great for making into semi-rigid shapes.

7. Suedette: totally synthetic to the touch, but does have really dense colour – see the African mask project on pages 52–53.

8. Handmade papers.

9. Synthetic organza gift bags (not pictured).

10. Knitted wire (not pictured).

11. Leaf skeletons: using them between layers of sheer fabrics can produce interesting results.

12. Flimsy plastic mesh.

13. Lightweight printed canvas shopping bags.

THINK BEFORE YOU BUY

As consumers, our appetite for beautiful fabrics seems to have no limits, and we also demand value for money. But how often do we stop to consider why a luxury item, for example a cashmere cardigan or silk blouse, can be bought in a supermarket or budget clothes store so inexpensively? Surely someone or something is paying the real price somewhere along the line?

All too often, it is workers toiling away in sweatshop conditions who bear the true cost, sometimes with their lives, as was the case at the Rana Plaza factory collapse in Bangladesh, in 2013. It isn't just humans who suffer though: the textile industry treats animals just as poorly. Silk worms are often boiled alive in order to release the silk fibre from their cocoons, and generally die in the process, while intensive angora rabbit farming frequently results in the animal's fur being cruelly ripped from its body.

But there is an alternative…

Fortunately there is a growing army of ethical textiles suppliers who take both the welfare of their workers and their animals seriously. Even big companies, such as yarn distributor Rowan, withdrew its angora haze range and replaced it with a more ethically sourced alternative. And there is good news for at least some silk worms. An ethical alternative to conventional silk is a product called *Ahimsa* (Sanskrit for 'do no harm') or 'peace silk'. The caterpillar is allowed to live out its natural life cycle, as the silk strand is extracted only after a metamorphosing worm has emerged from its cocoon.

COLOUR

Choosing colour can seem like a minefield of decisions, so it often feels safer simply to follow the tried and tested formulas laid out by others, rather than trust our instincts and try something we have a personal attachment to. Partly, this is because there are so many 'rules' surrounding the 'correct' use of colour that it can feel inhibiting to combine colours that aren't supposed to go together. But, for every ten designers and artists who apply colour in the 'correct' way there will be ten more who break the rules – with equally successful results.

Different colourways

Colour is such a personal matter and our tastes influenced by so many factors. Confident people might prefer bold vibrant colours; introverts muted colours. Context is all important too: for example, an exuberantly coloured Hawaiian shirt seems so right when set against a backdrop of golden sands, a deep blue sea and cloudless tropical sky, but looks out of place against the steel grey skies of a wintery day in Northern Europe! By using an assortment of colours and textures these three identical blocks suggest quite different moods:

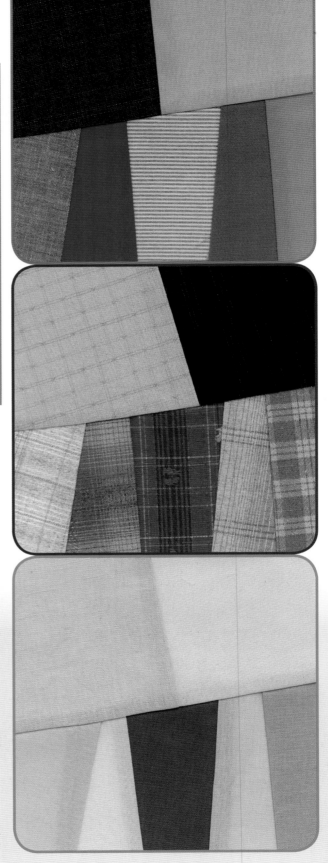

"Pink is the navy blue of India." – Diana Vreeland

Top: here saturated colours, old shirting, and denim off-cuts are combined to produce a block inspired by the Gee's Bend quilters of Alabama (see also pages 22–23).

Middle: tweeds or woven cloths that share a similar colour palette are ideal choices for primitive or rustic-looking textiles.

Bottom: muted hues and shades are good choices for colour schemes where you want to suggest cool and contemporary, shabby chic or beachcomber chic styles.

Colour at a glance

You could fill an entire library with books devoted to practical colour and colour theory. It's definitely worth investing in at least one book on colour theory, but for a (very) brief summary of the subject, and possible ways to use it, you might find the next few pages useful. Colour theory is there to help you and is a great starting point for when you're stuck for ideas but you should never be a slave to it. If there's a colour combination you particularly like, which doesn't comply with the rules, then throw away the rule book and be led by your own taste. And remember, just because someone else does it differently, it doesn't mean they are right and you are wrong.

The colour wheel

Primary (P): red, blue, yellow – colours that can't be mixed from any other colours.

Secondary (S): purple, green, orange – colours obtained by mixing two primary colours together.

Tertiary (T): these are obtained by mixing either one primary with a secondary, or two secondary colours together.

Variations of these basic twelve colours are obtained by adding quantities of black and white to them. A colour with white added to it is referred to as a **tint**, colour with black added to it is known as a **shade**.

Elsewhere...
- Quilter Nancy Crowe's bold use of colour
- Photographer Madame Yvonde's almost surrealistic use of colour

THE QUILTERS OF GEE'S BEND

In a remote part of the American deep south, hemmed in on three sides by the Alabama river, exists a community of quilters who produce work of extraordinary beauty. Their quilts display an innate sense of composition, balance and design, as well as a confidence with colour that rivals many of the great abstract expressionist painters. Yet until relatively recently, what have since come to be regarded as among the finest examples of African American textile art were largely unknown to anyone beyond Gee's Bend.

Who are the Gee's Bend quilters?

The quilters of Gee's Bend are the descendents of slaves who worked a cotton plantation belonging to Mark Pettway. Even after the abolition of slavery, many Gee's Bend residents chose to use the Pettway surname and continued to live in the area, scratching out a living as sharecroppers. The Gee's Bend community was dirt poor, cut off from the world at large because of its remote location, and a lack of access to the education and employment that most of us take for granted. This isolation proved to be both a blessing and curse. A curse because it led to disenfranchisement – many residents left their community in order make a life elsewhere. But ironically – considering their heritage – for those who stayed, isolation led to a freedom of creative expression unencumbered by trends in traditional quilting, which often prize perfection above creativity and flair. Isolation has also led to a unique continuity in quilt making, where the work of successive generations can be found all in one place.

My way

A Gee's Bend quilt doesn't follow the rules of conventional patchwork, and its aesthetic is a world away from that which considers adept fussy cutting and perfectly matched points the hallmark of an accomplished patchworker. Theirs is a far more improvisational approach that is partly driven by what fabrics are available, but also by what feels and looks right to the maker. The makers aren't afraid to use big blocks of colour and lines that aren't straight; artistic expression is paramount, so unusual rhythms occur in many of the designs. It is easy to see how the Gee's Bend aesthetic has influenced the Modern Quilt Movement, and its love of unstructured blocks and free cutting. There are, however, some designs that are common among the makers, the most obvious being 'housetops'. This is based on a series of concentric squares, which echo the outer border of the quilt and may bring to mind the 'call and response' of traditional African American songs.

The clothes on their backs

The fabrics that went in to making early Gee's Bend quilts included aprons, work dresses, plaid shirts and dungarees, as well as bleached feed sacks – basically any fabric that came to hand. After the Freedom Quilting Bee (a sewing cooperative with links to the civil rights movement) secured a contract with Sears, Roebuck & Co, to produce corduroy cushion covers, scraps of corduroy made their way into the quilts.

It is the clothes that tell the most heartbreaking stories though, as the extreme poverty of the residents meant their worldly belongings rarely amounted to anything more than the clothes on their backs. Quilts therefore came to have a sentimental value – as explained by Arizona Pettway: the day after her father died, Arizona's mother turned his old clothes into a quilt 'just to think about him for love' so that she would have something to remember him by. Even the stains in his work clothes, made from kneeling while picking potatoes, made it into the quilt.

The US postal service created a range of stamps in honour of the Gee's Bend quilts in 2006; Medallion by Loretta Pettway (left) and Bars and String-Pieced Columns by Jessie T. Pettway (right).

Recognition and opportunity

During the 1960s and 1970s, Gee's Bend quilts were *the* thing to have. Style maven and *Vogue* editor Diana Vreeland was a fan of them, while upmarket retailer Bloomingdales stocked them in its store. Sadly, it was a short-lived union as the quilters were uncomfortable with the demands of mass production, and Bloomingdales were unhappy with the irregularity of the quilts.

Then, in the late 1990s, curator, writer and collector Bill Arnett, fascinated by a Gee's Bend quilt he had seen, made the journey to Atlanta. His arrival was met with bemusement: residents were used to selling their quilts for a few dollars here and there, but he was offering a minimum of $250 a piece! Furthermore, he proclaimed that the same quilts would one day hang on gallery walls and change the lives of their makers forever.

Arnett was proved right, and in 2002 an exhibition of Gee's Bend quilts toured America. The resulting income funded the Gee's Bend Cooperative, which enables quilters to market their quilts and teach others their skills. Interest in Gee's Bend continues to this day and there are plans for visitor centres, improved housing and community projects that will benefit the lives of residents.

Elsewhere...
Compare the work of painters Frank Stella, Josef Albers and Mark Rothko with that of Gee's Bend quilters such as Jessie Pettway, Annie Mae Young and Arizona Pettway, to name just a few.

"Sewing is a job, but quilting is a joy!" – Essie Pettway

ALTERED IMAGES

Not everyone possesses an innate sense of perfect colour – some of us have to work harder at it. So if you need a little extra help, this exercise aims to boost your confidence when it comes to analysing and selecting palettes for textile projects.

As well as being a good exercise for developing your skills in handling colour, this is also a great way to start thinking of how you can abstract an image, rather than depict it literally. Start by selecting an image you like – in this case, one that appeals to you for its colour; I chose a white-and-red flower (shown below). Then using phone or computer software, pixellate that image. I used a mosaic filter that comes with Adobe Photoshop©, and pushed the strength right up as I didn't want the finished sample to be recognisable as a flower. Now, print out the pixellated image and use it as a chart so you can replicate it on canvas. Don't expect to create a perfect imitation, especially if using thread, as the colour choice will be more limited than the range produced by a printer. However, the exercise will encourage you to think about the colours you see, as well as develop your skill at matching and combining colours.

You will need

Stranded embroidery thread
  (four strands at a time)

Tapestry needle

14ct canvas

You could use

Chunkier threads, such as knitting yarn, on tapestry canvas, fabric swatches from your stash, or even scraps of paper

Tip

To add depth, and to avoid colours looking flat, have one thread in a slightly darker or lighter shade than the other three.

From source inspiration to chart to satin stitched colour palette.

Elsewhere...

• Pablo Picasso's analogous colours in *Man with the Blue Guitar*
• George Seurat's *Sunday Afternoon on the Island of La Grand Jatte* for its use of complementary colour
• Pauline Burbidge's quilts for her skilful use of monochromatic colour

What is a colour palette?

A colour palette is a set of colours grouped together to form a type of visual ambience. There are numerous to choose from but here are some of the most common:

- **Warm:** bold and energetic colours, found between the hot pinks and acid greens on a colour wheel. If you want colours that 'pop', this is where to go.

- **Cool:** colours that can be described as soothing. These colours will recede if placed against warmer colours, but also look great on their own.

- **Complementary:** colours opposite each other on the colour wheel, such as yellow and violet. Some skill is required in handling these colours, as they can be overwhelming – especially if you use them at full saturation.

- **Monochromatic:** when you take one basic colour but use different tints, shades and tones of that colour. Monochromatic palettes can look a bit bland, but an accent of a contrasting colour will often lift the overall scheme. Look at *boro* textiles to see some great examples of how an accent of colour (usually red) brings an otherwise plain scheme to life.

- **Analagous:** a combination of two or three colours found very close to each other on the colour wheel. Generally a fairly safe bet when it comes to selecting a palette!

- **Triadic:** when you have a combination of three, evenly spaced colours on the colour wheel, the most obvious of which would be red, blue and yellow. These combinations work best when you allow one of the three colours to dominate and the other two to play a supporting role.

An example of a cool, monochromatic palette but with additional pink accents to stop the scheme appearing too samey.

An example of hot, analagous colours: note how the complementary background greens help push the reds forward.

This triadic palette breaks down to colours that can be found in the red–violet, yellow–orange and blue–green part of the tertiary colour wheel. The blues and reds act almost as accents against the creamy yellows, which take up almost half the image.

"I never met a colour I didn't like." – Dale Chihuly

TONING IT DOWN

There is something about fabric shopping that brings out the 'child in a sweet shop' in all but the most self-disciplined of us. The result is that purchases that might have seemed like a good idea at the time end up looking busy and mismatched when combined in a textile. Don't worry though – here is a trick for toning down a piece of work that looks out of control: start by making yourself a nice cup of tea…

1. These leftover hexagons are from the first patchwork quilt I ever made. My original intention was to make a quilt that harked back to the days when every scrap was saved and put to good use elsewhere. Mistakenly, I used too many prints in too many colours and the result was quite dizzying! I should have remembered that less is more!

2. I painted over the more vibrant areas with a solution of bleach mixed with water. This isn't a precise science and results can't be predicted, so I just had to hope for the best… Fortunately, the dark purples, browns, greys and greens, which particularly bothered me, responded well to the bleach and faded quite well. I avoided delicate fabrics, such as the vintage silk, as these would have disintegrated had bleach been applied to them. When I was happy with the result, I thoroughly rinsed the fabric to stop the bleach doing any more work.

3. I then soaked the fabrics in a solution of tea. Soak the fabric for about thirty minutes, before removing from the solution, rinsing and leaving to dry. The tea solution gives the piece an overall muted tone.

4. To fake my antique further, I snipped away at some of the cloth and backed it with scraps of fabric I'd used in the original patchwork. Finally, a little bit of stitching and darning helps create the illusion of a worn and much-loved heirloom textile.

"Good artists copy, great artists steal..." – Pablo Picasso

How to choose colour

- Save the selvedges from any fabrics you buy – they contain a series of coloured dots that reference the designer's colour palette. If you particularly like the colour palette, use the selvedge to select similar colours for other projects. Or use the selvedge to select accent colours that go well with the original fabric.

- Carry a roll of sticky tape around with you. When I see a pleasingly coloured rogue clump of threads in my sewing room, I pick them up with a piece of sticky tape and stick it in my sketchbook – hey presto, a ready-made palette! This works just as well with snippets of card, powdered make-up, dried flecks of chipped paint and helps with the tidying up too!

- While it's easy to get sidetracked by sites like Pinterest, they are useful for compiling moodboards. There's no limit to how many boards you can have so you could devote a board to every colour under the sun!

Tip

Painting fabric with lemon juice and leaving it out in the sun lightens it. You could also try rubbing areas with sandpaper to tone down prints that are too dominant.

"Our lives are like quilts - bits and pieces, joy and sorrow, stitched with love." – Anon

STRAIGHT AHEAD: RUNNING STITCHES

Simple, straight stitching can be as versatile and expressive as handwriting – neat and orderly sewers tend to make their stitches likewise; expansive personalities will produce bigger and bolder stitches. Neither is better, both are good; just make your style work for you.

EXPLORING STRAIGHT STITCHES

There's so much more to straight stitches than running stitch…

Running stitches

Using different coloured thread for simple, ordered stitches can make an elegant statement.

Stitching into tweed

Accentuate the beauty of tweed by adding lines of running stitch in the same colours used in the cloth.

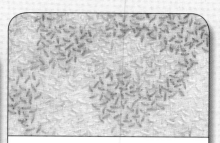

Seed stitch

Seed stitch makes a wonderful background filler, and can be worked small or large. But whether working large or small, keep the size of your stitches consistent.

Mohair snowflake

Mohair, metallic thread and sequins are used to make a pretty snowflake.

Tension

Play around with tension. Rather than working with a single thread and a consistent tension, here the thread is doubled and the tension is deliberately inconsistent: sometimes taut, sometimes creating loops that are decorated with seed beads.

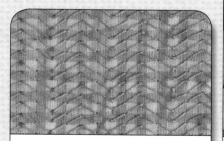

Changing direction

I started with seven columns of long stitches, then pulled down the centre of one stitch to align with the stitch below and couched it in place with a contrasting colour. Changing direction from column to column results in a wave effect.

Satin stitch

Satin stitch – tightly packed straight stitch – is ideal for completely covering a background.

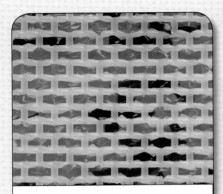

Plastic bags

Shredded plastic bags can easily be turned into 'thread'.

Knitting yarn

Yarn has been sewn through this builders' mesh – an interesting result is achieved simply by following its diagonal lines.

Fringing

Instead of tying off ends, let them dangle to create a fringe or perhaps a jelly fish.

Sewing on paper

Try sewing straight lines on paper or card: vary the length and direction of stitches to create eye-catching string drawings.

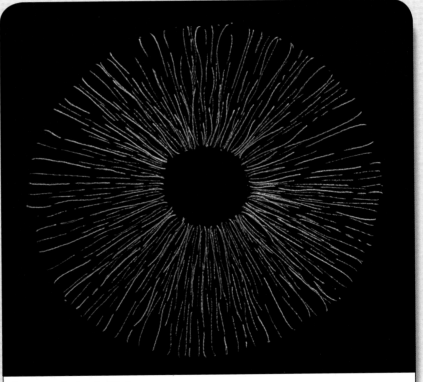

Long and short stitch

Masses of metallic threads were used on a suedette background to suggest an exploding firework.

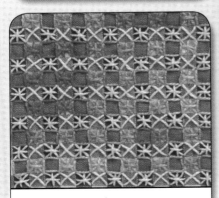

Chicken scratch

Chicken scratch – an old-school favourite – is charming and easy to do. Best of all, the gingham background provides a perfect gauge for measuring your stitches.

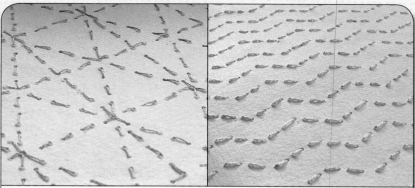

Sewing into paper

When sewing into paper, you can always pre-pierce it with a needle, awl or even a sewing machine to obtain perfect spacing. You might even find this helps with other hand stitching, as with practice you'll become familiar with the rhythm of evenly spaced stitches.

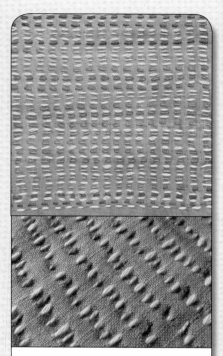

Shibori

A layer of *shibori*-dyed lawn is sewn with *kantha* style stitching (top) to this piece of linen (bottom) that was dyed with onion skins, to create a *dorukha,* which is a traditional form of Indian sewing where the fabric is reversible and the pattern is the same when viewed from both sides.

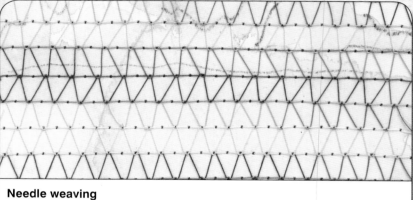

Needle weaving

Thread woven between rows of running stitches creates an interesting pattern.

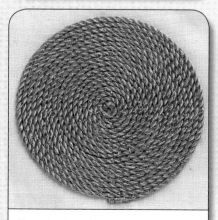

Couched patch

Here, gold cord has been couched onto a background and can now be cut out and used as an appliqué patch.

Boro preservation

Be inspired by *boro* – layer upon layer of straight stitches preserve a piece of fabric that has worn thin with use.

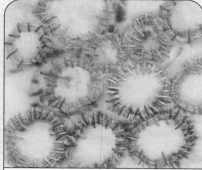

Couching yarn

Circles were painted onto fabric, over which loops of yarn were roughly couched in place with big, bold stitches.

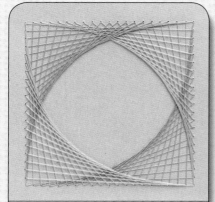

Parabolic curves

With careful spacing, straight lines can even make parabolic curves (see also pages 56–57).

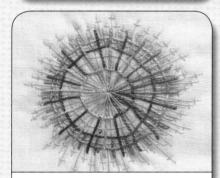

Decorative tacking

Mennonite tacks of different lengths are worked around concentric circles to create a kaleidoscopic effect (see page 147).

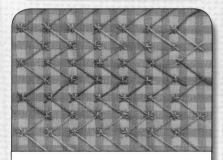

Decorative zigzags

Long, diagonal stitches that overlap as they change direction are embellished with small cross stitches.

Darn it

Darning doesn't need to be discreet: try weaving a contrast colour through the warp threads to make a decorative feature of your mending.

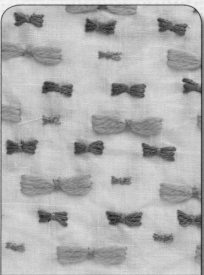

Cinched threads

Groups of three closely spaced running stitches are cinched together at the centre with tiny cross stitches. A variety of embroidery threads and scraps of leftover knitting yarn have been used.

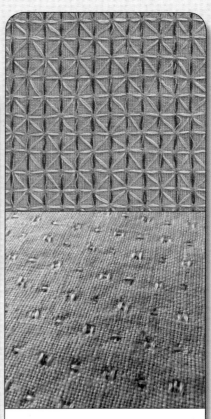

Sashiko

This colourful *sashiko* looks good from the front (top) and the back (bottom).

Criss cross

Random, wonky crosses of different sizes add structure and a contrasting texture to the softness of the felt background.

LOVELY JUBBLY

When I was little, one of my favourite summer treats was a Jubbly™. For anyone who hasn't heard of them (and has therefore missed out on one of life's great pleasures) a Jubbly™ was a brightly coloured, tetrahedron-shaped carton filled with a fruity ice lolly. These paper packages are inspired by this but are filled with colourful candies rather than ice lollies. With a different choice of paper however, and filled with sugared almonds, these would make lovely wedding favours.

You will need

Sheets of medium-weight card measuring 18 x 13cm (7 x 5in)

Any brightly coloured threads, such as cotton perlé

Basic sewing kit

Sewing machine (optional)

Ruler (optional)

Pencil (optional)

Large needle or awl (optional)

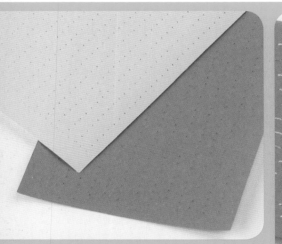

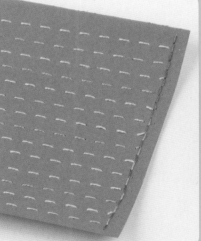

1. If you are using a sewing machine, set the stitch length to its longest length and sew lines roughly 8mm (⅓in) apart down the length of the card, stopping 1cm (½in) short at either end of the card. Sew a line of holes across the top and bottom of the card 1cm (½in) in from each end. Of course, you can do this by hand using a ruler and pencil to mark out your lines and a pin, or awl, to perforate the lines, but it will take longer.

2. Sew through all the perforated lines with brightly coloured threads.

3. Fold the shorter ends to the wrong side so that the lines of stitching are on the folded edge. Bring these edges together so the card forms a tube, then whip stitch, along the lines of running stitch, to hold the tube together.

5. To form the tetrahedron shape, pinch the opposite sides of the tube together. So, let's say you pinched north and south together in the last step, you now need to pinch the east and west sides of the tube together, to form the tetrahedron. Sew the end as in step 4; choose whether or not to firmly knot the threads: if you do, you'll have to tear the packages open to get at the contents, if you don't, the thread can simply be whipped out to open the package. If doing the latter, you could add a little tag, labelled 'pull me' to the end of the thread...

4. Flatten and pinch one end of the tube together and sew the sides together.

6. If you like, trim the edges of the packages with scalloped or pinking shears.

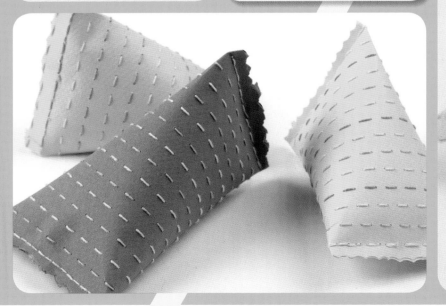

POJAGI PATCHWORK

A *pojagi* is a traditional wrapping cloth from Korea. Usually made from silk, it has a translucent quality that when held up to the light resembles stained glass windows.

The beauty of a *pojagi* panel lies in its composition, and composition is all about balance. When used skilfully, composition directs the viewer's eye exactly where the designer wants it to. A good way to understand the basic rules of composition is to look at the golden section. Also known as the golden ratio, the golden section has fascinated artists, philosophers and mathematicians for over 2,400 years.

Think about it… Most images, be they adverts in magazines, works of art – realistic or abstract – tend to use some kind of golden section composition. It could be just a subtle colour shift (particularly in an abstract image), or it might be a direct positioning of an object – such as the horizon in a landscape painting. Sometimes, art directors deliberately mess about with composition – particularly in advertising – to create an image that flouts the rules to shock and hold the viewer's attention. So when designing a textile, think about whether you want a soothing, balanced effect, or something that jars – but deliberately so, because you're in control of and understand the rules of composition.

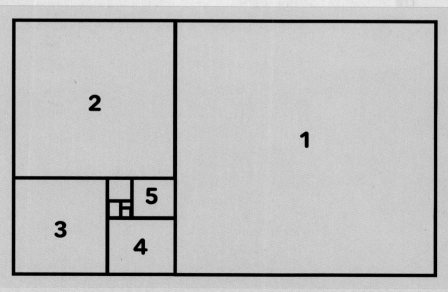

THE GOLDEN SECTION

The basic division of the rectangle is that the largest area (1) takes up roughly two-thirds of the total area. Now, if you exclude 1, the second largest area (2) takes up roughly two-thirds of the remaining area, and so on ad infinitum!

MAKING A POJAGI PATCHWORK

This panel follows the golden section; to make one you'll need

At least 1m (39in) of organdie, silk or organza

Thread in a toning colour

Basic sewing kit

Preparing your fabrics

Cut your fabric according to the template on page 152, or create your own golden rectangle pattern (NB: this may affect how much fabric you need). You will start by sewing the smallest pieces together first, then the next smallest, joining the largest piece last of all. If there is excess fabric on the larger piece, after joining the smaller pieces to it, simply trim it away. I used regular French seams to construct this panel – if you've done any dressmaking, you're probably familiar with this technique already.

French seams

1. Place two fabric pieces wrong sides together and seam using a 9mm (³/₈in) seam allowance. Trim the seam to 5mm (¼in). Open the seam so the right side of fabric is facing you and press the seam to one side. Turn the fabric over and press the seam from the other side.

2. Bring the fabric pieces right sides together, fold along the line of stitching, then press.

3. Pin in place and sew another seam, along the same joined edge, using a 9mm (³/₈in) seam allowance. The original seam will now be trapped inside this new seam.

4. Press the seam flat. You can either leave the seam as it is or, if you prefer, sew the seam along its edge, which is something you might want to do for a *pojagi* patchwork. You might even decide to make a decorative feature of the stitching by using a contrasting thread.

Elsewhere...

- Laszlo Mohly-Nagy's KVII for *pojagi* inspiration
- Virtually any painting by Salvador Dali, as he was obsessed by the golden section

INTENTIONALLY RANDOM

Just as it takes practice and flair to successfully pull off the elegantly dishevelled look – and not look like you've been dragged through a hedge backwards – making a random pattern with your stitches appear effortless really requires method and a clear idea of the effect you're trying to create. When creating a background pattern of dots, an illustrator might draw intersecting clusters of dots or dashes to gradually fill up an area. They wouldn't just start by doing one dot in, say, the top left-hand corner of the page, another at the base, then another on the right-hand edge and so on, as it simply wouldn't create a natural and convincing-looking pattern. The same applies to stitching. A good way to appreciate this way of working is to try the following exercise…

You will need

Fabric of your choice

Jam jar with lid

Rice

Cold-water dye and some water

Dye fixative (optional)

A fork

Basic sewing kit

Thread: I used stranded embroidery cotton

"All my scattering moments are taken up with my needle." –
Ellen Birdseye Wheaton

1. Fill a jar with some rice grains, some dye and a little bit of water. If you want to keep the colour of the dye, add a fixative to the solution; if you want the dye to disappear, make sure you use something that will eventually wash out. Be careful not to add too much water, or the rice will turn into a soggy mess. Spraying the water into the jar, rather than adding it from the tap, helps you control how wet the mixture gets. Run a fork through the rice grains to keep them separated.

2. Place an object, such as the lid of a jar, on some fabric, then pour the still-wet grains of rice around the lid. Let the grains fall naturally, and don't be tempted to 'tidy' everything up.

3. When the rice grains are completely dry, remove them and the lid, and you should be left with a pattern to follow.

4. Start by stitching a tiny row of backstitches around the edge of the negative space, then begin to work outwards from the backstitch with seed stitch. The trick with seed stitch is to place one stitch at roughly 45° to the last, and to avoid having the stitches parallel to each other. Continue to fill in the area made by the dyed rice grains, using darker thread where the colour is most condensed, and a lighter thread where the colour is weakest. It's absolutely fine to work over the darker areas with stitches in threads of similar tone, as this will help make these areas look even more condensed.

The finished sample has a greater concentration of stitches at the centre, while stitches get sparser the further away they are.

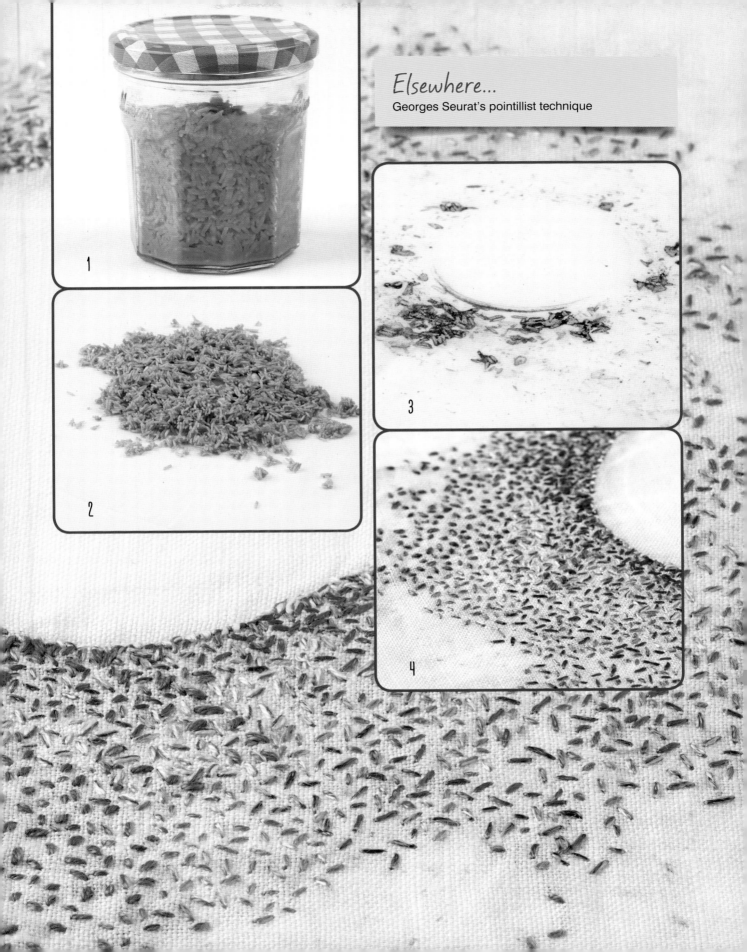

1

2

3

4

KANTHA FISHES

If I was restricted to only one style of sewing for the rest of my life, it would be *kantha*. *Kantha*, which originates from South Asia, and in Sanskrit means 'rags', is one of the humblest forms of stitching. Rather like Japanese *boro* textiles (see pages 42–43), *kantha* was often created from an economic need to preserve cloth rather than a desire simply to decorate and adorn. As with *boro* textiles, the fine rows of tiny running stitches result in a delightful puckering of the fabric. However, *kantha* can be used more playfully than *boro* and it is quite common to see decorative motifs such as themes from folklore and nature, or even pictorial narratives of the maker's hopes and desires, added to saris or thin, two-sided quilts also known as *kantha dorukha*. For this small piece of *kantha* I've created an abstract shoal of shimmering fish, but the design could easily be adapted to suggest an autumnal theme of falling leaves.

You will need

Two pieces of linen measuring 34 x 25cm (13½ x 10in)
An assortment of small organza gift bags
Gold metallic thread
Cotton perlé thread

1. Tack/baste the two layers of linen together. Cut out five or more leaf shapes from organza – make them roughly 7.5cm (3in) long and 5cm (2in) wide. Pin the shapes to the fabric, arranging them so that some overlap, and the design suggests a shoal of swimming fish.

2. Sew around the edges of each fish shape with running stitch using gold metallic thread.

3. Apply a few more fish shapes to the background. Place some so that they overlap the shimmery fishes; have others solely on the linen background. Sew around these new fish with metallic thread.

4. Using matt thread, such as cotton perlé, sew around the outer edge of the shoal of fish with tiny little running stitches. Try to keep your stitch length even and avoid making increasingly longer stitches as you work outward to the edge of your frame.

Tip

Have an odd number of fish on your background. Aesthetically, this is more pleasing to the eye than an even number of shapes.

BORO TEXTILES

As evidence of what many regarded to be a shameful reminder of Japan's feudal past, *boro* textiles might have slipped quietly into a forgotten corner of history, had it not been for the foresight of a few dedicated collectors. Thanks to them, the cultural value of *boro* textiles has since been recognised. *Boro* decorates the walls of countless cool urban interiors and has influenced fashion designers such as Alexander McQueen, and Junya Watanabe at Comme des Garçons.

Meaning 'tattered cloth', *boro* textiles were literally that. Layers of indigo-dyed cotton scraps sewn together with running stitch, *boro* textiles are testament to the severity of Japan's past sumptuary laws. Seeking to preserve social hierarchies, sumptuary laws forbade lower classes from trying to appear 'better than they were'. The merchant classes, for example, even if they could afford fine clothing, were forbidden from dressing better than the Samurai classes, as they were thought to contribute less to society. Farmers – also non-Samurai – were forbidden from wearing silk even if they harvested and dyed it, as silk could only be worn by nobles.

In reality, sumptuary laws were pointless, since the peasant classes could barely afford the cost of cotton, ramie or hemp for their clothes and household furnishings – never mind silk! However, while an economic need to preserve cloth was certainly a characteristic of *boro*, another characteristic is clear: '*mottainai*', which means a sense of regret about wastefulness – a waste not, want not approach.

This putting to use of something that is too good to waste is, for me, what makes *boro* textiles so appealing. Knowing this means that when I look at genuine *boro* textiles, I see something that was made with skill, and a deliberate sense of design – not just the result of a happy accident. Although *boro* items are utilitarian and the layers of fabric and rows of tiny *sashiko* stitching there for purposes of repair and insulation, they are also objects of beauty and demonstrate an appreciation for textiles by the maker.

While Japan is hardly unique in having a rich tradition for preserving its textiles and passing them down from one generation to the next, *boro* items in particular are often a tangible link between the current holder and their ancestors. The *bodoko*, for example, which translates as 'life-cloth', was an every day bedsheet used also during childbirth. As it was the first thing the baby touched when it came into the world, the baby would be linked to its ancestors by having contact with the scraps of cloth they had once worn. Indeed, human contact was vital for keeping warm during the harsh Japanese winters; entire families would sleep naked inside a *donja*, an enormous, heavy, sleeping coat, made from layers of *boro* scraps. This might seem shocking to some, yet it underlines how important *boro* textiles were to their owners – not just for clothing the body, or furnishing the home – but also the role cloth played in binding generations together. The image above right shows a selection of work clothes and sleeping kimonos.

Elsewhere...

- Georges Seurat's pointillist technique
- Traditional *boro* items: futons, fishermen's jackets, *bodokos*, *donjas*
- *Boro*-inspired fashion: see also Alexander McQueen, Comme de Garçons and Paromita Banerjee (see right)

BORO-INSPIRED TEXTILES

Boro inspires many contemporary fashion designers, including Paromita Banerjee, whose Autumn/Winter 2015 collection addresses the idea of 'too good to waste' by exploring, recycling and upcycling fabric wastes and creating value out of leftovers (see right). Naturally-dyed handwoven *khadi* fabrics are at the heart of the collection, which explores layers of textiles (from four different weaving clusters), textures and techniques. One versatile example is the quintessential Indian *kurta* that becomes a 'tunic' when worn with stockings in the West but, when worn with a *dupatta* and *churidar* in the East, becomes 'traditional and homely' – allowing a woman to celebrate her cultural ethos.

VISIBLE MENDING

A much-loved but torn and moth-eaten textile needn't
be thrown away or left on a mending pile that never gets
tackled. Neither should signs of mending be something to
be embarrassed by. Think instead of darning as a feature
that can add texture and decoration to textiles.

1. Using a water-soluble pen,
   draw a shape around the
   damaged area (I drew around
   an egg cup). Draw vertical
   lines across the shape to
   serve as a guide for where to
   sew the warp threads.

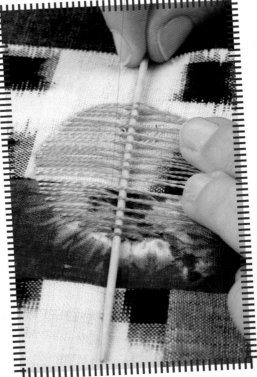

2. Use a regular needle to sew your warp threads. Aim for a
   consistent distance between the threads from top to bottom, and
   (unless you want your darning to be deliberately wonky), make
   sure they are parallel with the hang, or drape, of your textile.

3. Weave a cocktail stick or small
   double pointed needle through the
   warp threads, over then under, over
   then under, until you get to the end
   of the row. Push the stick to the top
   of the work; you will use it to beat
   down the weft threads as you work.
   Separating alternative warp threads
   with a stick will also help you keep
   track of your stitches and how they
   need to be worked.

"A stitch in time saves nine..." – Anon

4. Thread a tapestry needle with a long length of thread and beginning with the central three * stitches weave your needle in between the warp threads as indicated by the diagram below. Exactly when you take in more warp threads will depend on your shape, but the crucial point to remember is that any new stitch must be worked in the opposite manner to the previous stitch. For example, if the needle went over the last thread, it has to go under the next (new) thread, so when you change direction the order of weaving continues to alternate from one row to the next.

*How many threads you pick up will vary depending on the shape of your darning. On an extremely graduated shape, like an oval, you probably will pick up only three threads, but on something with a flatter base, it could be more.

Follow the chart

1st row
Working right to left, over 1, under 0, over -1.

2nd row
Working from left to right, under -1, over 0, under 1.

3rd row (increase)
Working right to left, under 2, over 1, under 0, over -1, under -2.

4th row
Working left to right, over -2, under -1, over 0, under 1, over 2.

5th row (increase)
Working right to left, over 3, under 2, over 1, under 0, over -1, under -2, over -3.

6th row
Working from left to right, under -3, over -2, under -1, over 0, under 1, over 2, under 3 and so on…

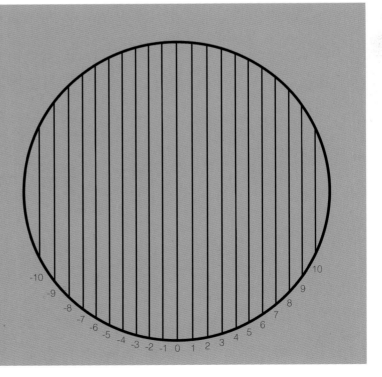

A LEAF OUT OF MY BOOK

Sweet and simple, saddle-stitched notebooks are easy to make. I keep one in virtually every bag I own – you never know when inspiration will strike and you need to jot down an idea!

"I spend a lot of time preparing. I think a lot about what I want to do. I have prep books, little notebooks in which I write everything down before a sitting. Otherwise I would forget my ideas." – Helmut Newton

Making the cover

I wanted to show off the flowers in this handmade paper and not hide them between the pages…

1. Match up the front cover with the position of one of the petals on the first inside page. You will cut a 'window' in the cover to frame this petal, so draw a line over where the petal sits. Draw a leaf shape over this line, to indicate where you will cut, then draw another leaf shape around this, about 3mm (^{1}/$_8$in) larger all round, to use a stitch guide. Do not draw the lines too heavily – you will need to erase them later. Using a set square, draw intersecting horizontal lines, 2–3mm (^{1}/$_{16}$–^{1}/$_8$in) apart, all the way along the vertical line, making sure to extend them beyond the outer border.

2. Cut out the inner shape.

3. Using an awl or needle, pierce where the lines cross the outer leaf shape. Note that the holes are pierced from the front of the card, as you want the raised tufts of paper, where the needle and thread exits, to be hidden at the back of your work. Also add a few more holes at the bottom for a stem.

4. Using some fine variegated cotton, sew across the back of the leaf, working from side to side.

Saddle-stitching

5. Mark five equally spaced points on the spine of the book. Clip the inside pages and cover together, centring the pages, so that they cannot move. Pierce the five holes through all layers.

6. Using a long length of waxed thread, take the needle down through C. Leave a long tail for knotting off when the stitching is complete. Bring it back up through point D, and back down through point E. Take it back up through point D, and back down through point B. Bring the needle up through point A. Take the needle down through point B and finish by bringing it back at C. Remove the needle and knot off initial and end tails of thread with a double knot. Trim to shortish tails and weave ends into stitching.

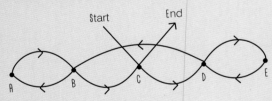

7. Bring the central pages together first, then the next set of pages, then the next, until all the pages fold together neatly. Fold the cover away from the inner pages (this sounds counterintuitive but helps to give the cover and spine more flexibility) before folding them together to cover the inside pages.

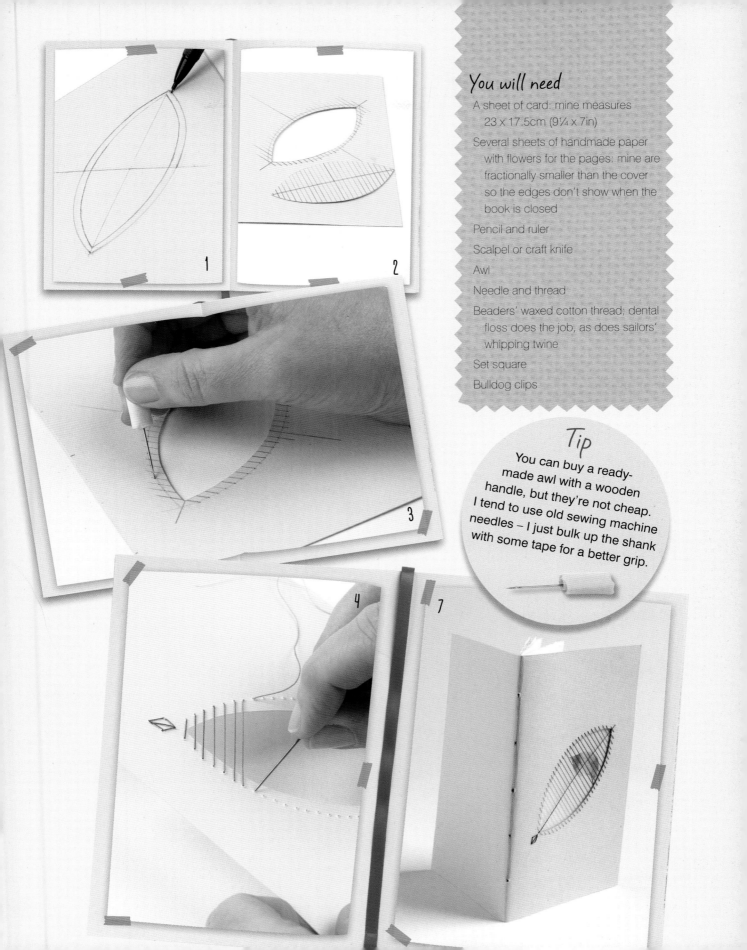

You will need

A sheet of card: mine measures 23 x 17.5cm (9¼ x 7in)

Several sheets of handmade paper with flowers for the pages: mine are fractionally smaller than the cover so the edges don't show when the book is closed

Pencil and ruler

Scalpel or craft knife

Awl

Needle and thread

Beaders' waxed cotton thread; dental floss does the job, as does sailors' whipping twine

Set square

Bulldog clips

Tip
You can buy a ready-made awl with a wooden handle, but they're not cheap. I tend to use old sewing machine needles – I just bulk up the shank with some tape for a better grip.

1

2

3

4

7

TYPE MATTERS!

Always consider your choice of fonts – you don't want to send out the wrong message.

We are confronted with thousands of typefaces on a daily basis. Each font does a different job, and conveys subtle yet effective messages when used well. If this wasn't the case, we would need only one font and use it on everything from Valentine's cards to death certificates (although the purist typographer in me would probably argue that Helvetica Neue could fulfil that purpose!)

For example, scripts work well on quality linen, as flourishes and swirls help to suggest elegance and a taste for the finer things in life. Slab serifs and bold sans serif fonts are perfect for sports wear, partly because they can be easily identified when in motion, but also because they suggest a no-nonsense attitude. Copperplate and, in particular, gothic fonts are ideal for religious vestments. While serifs, such as Times, are the obvious choice if you're trying to convey a classic, or traditional, image.

The artist Tracey Emin is well-known for using written messages in her work. Her quilts feature slogans and pithy comments in roughly cut-out fabrics that seem to be almost deliberately naive in their execution. Their overall effect however is bold and exciting while the juxtaposition of a traditional craft such as quilting with the artist's sometimes shocking pronouncements certainly grabs one's attention.

Genuinely naive, and completely charming are Portuguese love hankies. These were love tokens, sent by young girls to soldiers. Embroidered with symbols of love such as birds, hearts and flowers, the hankies also included messages (often full of spelling errors) and declarations of love for the recipient.

Elsewhere...
Tracey Emin's Tent: *Everyone I Have Ever Slept With*

"Typography is what language looks like." – Ellen Lupton

Elsewhere...
- Portuguese love hankies
- Home Sweet Home samplers
- Hell's Angels biker jackets
- The Bayeaux Tapestry
- Basketball jackets
- Football shirts

VARSITY LETTERS

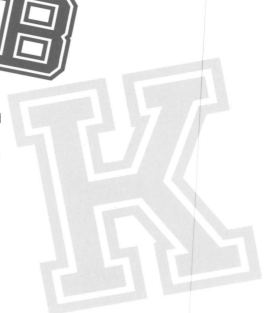

I wanted to sew some big and bold letters. First I thought about comic book sounds, such as 'wham' and 'kapow', then I looked at astronauts' mission badges. In the end, I was inspired by varsity letters and numbers found on baseball jackets and school sportswear.

You will need

A piece of linen large enough to accommodate my design, allowing for a 5cm (2in) border all the way around

Water-soluble cross-stitch canvas

Water-soluble pen

An embroidery hoop

Cotton perlé thread

Basic sewing kit

A lightbox (optional)

1. Print out your chosen letters – there are numerous resources for varsity letters online – and cut them out. Try creating a little moodboard of letters and words to help pin down your idea.

2. Play around with the composition until you're happy with it but don't over-complicate it. For example, note how I aligned the vertical line at the top left of the Y with the downstroke of the N, and filled in the gap between the N and Y – this helped to simplify the sewing.

3. Using a water-soluble pen and a lightbox, trace your design onto the linen. If you don't have a lightbox, see the tip box, above right, for a few alternative methods.

4. Place the water-soluble canvas on top of your design and clamp them in an embroidery hoop. In a contrasting thread (to the ones used for the embroidery) tack/baste the canvas and fabric together 1cm (½in) or so around the edges of your design. Fill in the design with your chosen colours, using cross stitches (see tip box, below right).

5. Now watch the magic happen: remove the work from the hoop and immerse it in a bowl of warm water. You may need to leave the fabric for a few hours. Both the canvas and pen marks will disappear before your eyes!

Tip

If you don't have a lightbox, tape your design, with the fabric over it, to a bright window and use this as a lightbox. Or, if you have a glass table, place a small bedside light under it and this will serve perfectly as a homemade lightbox.

2

3

4

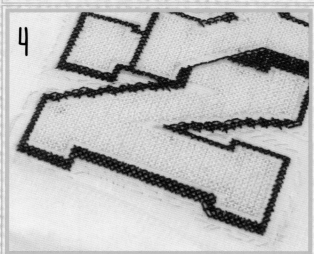

5

Tip

When working your stitches, don't be tempted to make one complete stitch at a time. Instead, working from left to right, work all the right-leaning strokes first, then go back to the beginning and do the left-leaning strokes. This will result in a neat finish and means the plastic embroidery canvas is much less likely to buckle.

AFRICAN MASK

The multi-faceted nature of African sculpture (where multiple viewpoints of the body can be seen at once) was a great influence on many early 20th-century artists and helped redefine how the human figure was represented in Western art. Part of the reason for its popularity was that many artists felt the old way of looking at things had become tired, and a new, radical way was needed to reflect the times. African art provided that; it possessed a sense of energy and movement, as well as being based on abstraction rather than literal interpretation. You can see its influence in Cubism and Picasso, who was a great collector of African art, may well have drawn inspiration from his collection of Grebo and Nimba masks when he created the sculptures of his mistress Marie-Thérèse during the 1930s.

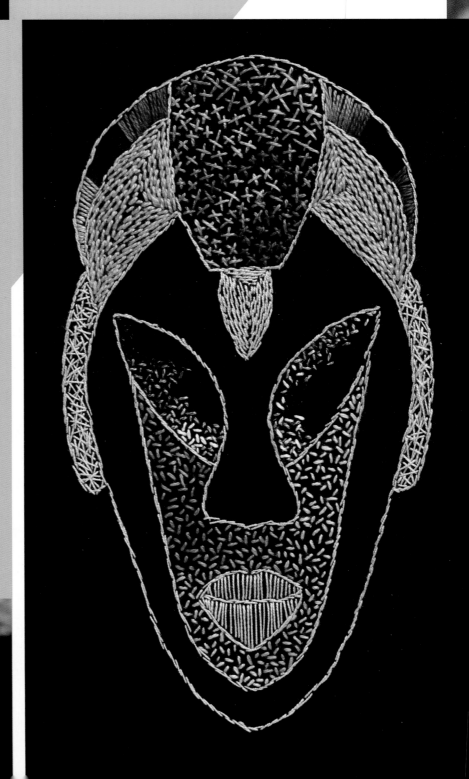

1. Start by creating a moodboard of images – it can include textures, fabric swatches, beads and even your own sketches.

2. You can use the mask template on page 152, but if you prefer to design your own mask, draw a vertical line on a sheet of paper and draw one half of the face.

3. Place the fusible interfacing over the paper and trace off your design. Flip the fusible interfacing, marry up the central vertical lines, and draw the other half of the face. Your drawing will now be completely symmetrical.

4. Iron the interfacing to the back of your fabric. Work with the reverse of the fabric facing you and backstitch the outline, with threads of your choice, making sure any knots remain on this side. You might find it helps to colour in the fusible interfacing then use this as a guide for selecting, and sticking to, your chosen colours.

5. Here you can see the design with the backstitched lines in place. Fill the planes with various straight stitches. The stitches don't have to be neat – in fact, a slightly 'rough' appearance might better suggest wood carving. I used cross stitches and stem stitch on the forehead, with regular, closely spaced straight stitch on the crown. I used wonky layered crosses on the ears and seed stitch on the cheeks to suggest scarification, then more straight stitches for the lips (refer to finished piece, opposite).

Elsewhere...

• Pablo Picasso's busts of Marie-Thérèse

• Picasso's *Head of a Woman*, 1907

• African masks

COLOURFUL CORDS

For sheer pizazz and exuberance, the work of Milton Glaser and his partner, Seymour Chwast, at Push Pin Studios can't be matched. As gifted an illustrator as he is a designer, Glaser produced some of the most iconic graphic images from the 1950–80s, such as the I ♥ NY campaign, and countless posters, most memorable of which must be the silhouetted profile of Bob Dylan, crowned with a colourful mass of undulating curls. I have always loved this poster, and it inspired me to create something similarly funky, but with fabric and thread rather than print.

© Milton Glaser

You will need

Two pieces of black felt measuring 29 x 22cm (11½ x 8²/₃in)

A variety of colourful elastic cords bought from a chandler's store

Black thread

Sewing machine with zipper foot

Elsewhere...
- Push Pin Studios
- Sol Lewitt's colourful wall drawings, especially *Wall Drawing #1136*

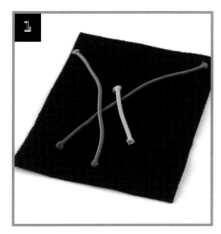

1. Decide on your design, perhaps draw it out on paper first, then cut the cords into appropriate lengths, allowing for extra to be sandwiched between the layers of felt, and so that every length of cord is long enough to reach the edge of the felt.

2. Make small slits in one piece of felt and thread the cords through until the concealed end reaches the edge of felt. It's important to do this, as otherwise when you come to encase the cords, baggy, half-filled channels will look as if you've miscalculated the cord lengths.

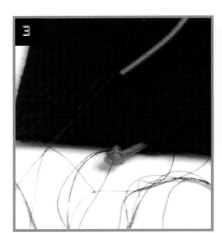

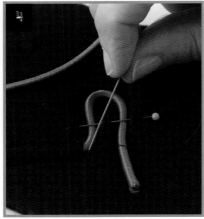

3. Lay this piece on top of another piece of felt and pin in place to make a 'cord sandwich'. Using a zipper foot, sew as close as you can through the layers of felt along the concealed sides of the cords. Leave really long tails of thread – you will use these to sew the cords into curves in the next step.

4. Curve the cords according to your design and sew them in place. As you sew the cords in place, don't just think of the shape the curved line will make. Also think of the shapes that will be created in the background. These are called the negative spaces and they are as important to the overall design as the linework itself.

ONE STITCH, THREE STEPS

Each time you sew a bit of the cord to the felt, don't be tempted to try and do it all in one go. Instead, break the task down into three actions:

1. Bring up your needle through the felt.

2. Catch the back of the cord.

3. Take the needle back down through the felt. It takes longer, but gives a better result, with less likelihood of pricking yourself!

STRING THEORY

I was once told that sewing is basically applied mathematics. However, if maths was your most-hated subject at school, don't panic or be put off by this exercise that shows you how to produce a parabolic curve with straight lines. The technique is so easy to master that you'll soon be spinning and repeating the X/Y-axis to produce your own dazzlingly impressive, yet deceptively simple string drawings.

You will need

Fabric or card
Thread of your choice
A ruler
A set square
Water-soluble pen

1. With a water-soluble pen, draw a grid as shown below right. You can make the grid as large or small as you like, but a smaller grid will be easier to work with and use up less thread. Bring your needle up through number 15 on the Y-axis, then take it to the back of your work through number 1 on the X-axis. Bring your needle up through 14 on the Y-axis and take it to the back of your work through number 2 on the X-axis. Repeat until you reach the end of the line (13–3, 12–4, 11–5 and so on).

2. Do exactly as you've just done in the previous step, but this time you'll be working from -15 to -1 and -14 to -2.

3. Work the other two areas in exactly the same way, turning your work as you go.

4. To create a second layer, simply rotate the grid 45° clockwise, and repeat using a different thread.

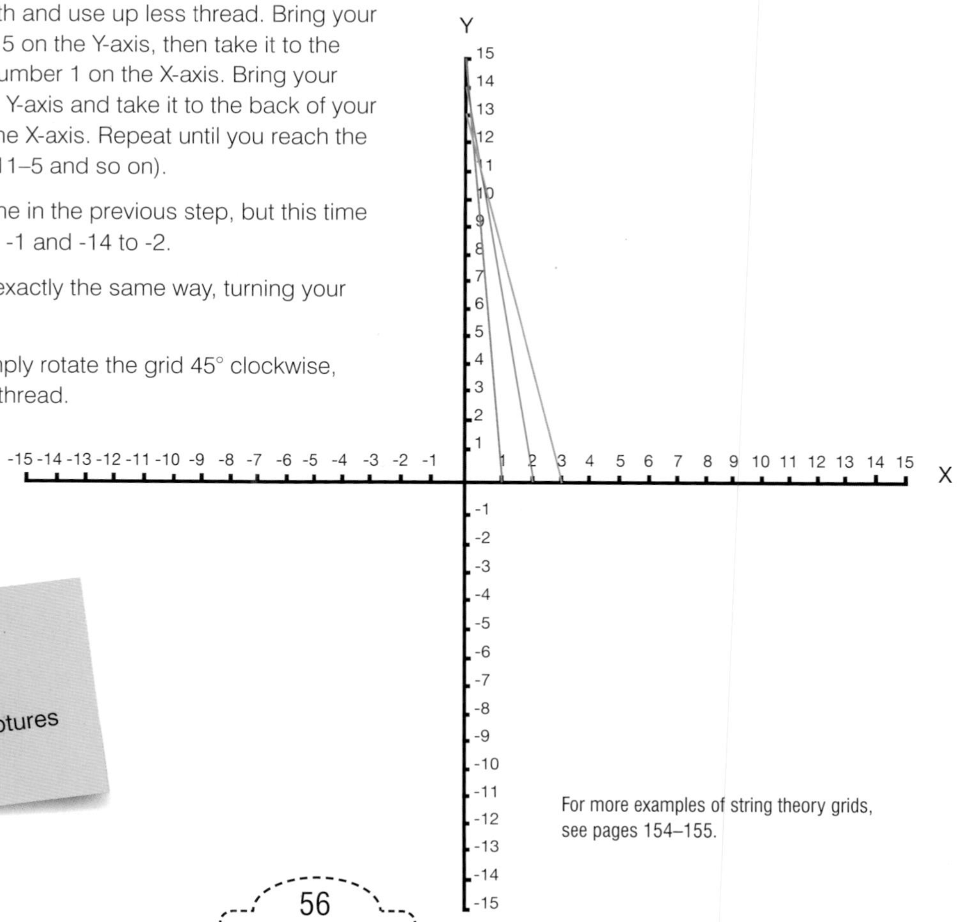

Elsewhere...
Naum Gabo's string sculptures

For more examples of string theory grids, see pages 154–155.

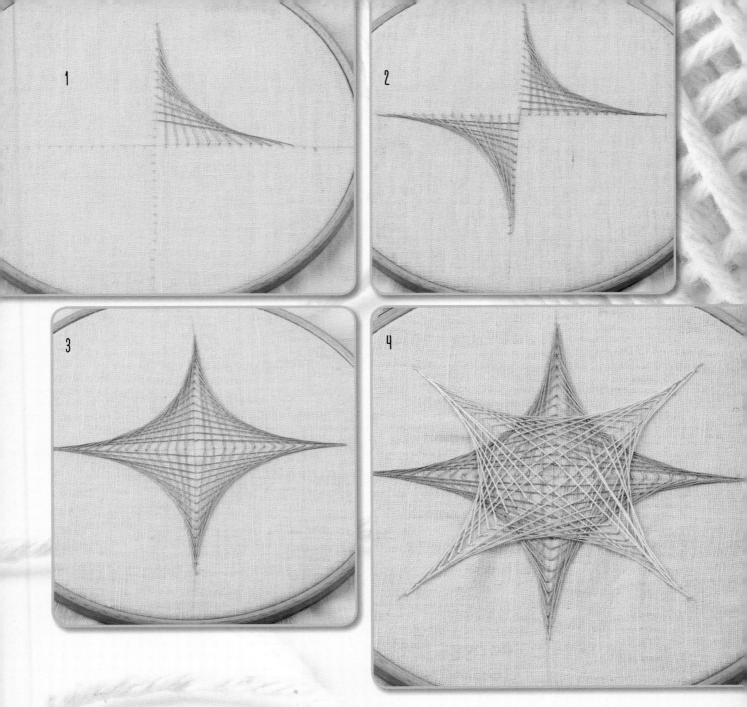

1

2

3

4

Tip

You might find it helps to rotate your work as you go, so the section you are working is always in the upper right-hand side (although, if left-handed, you might prefer it with the working area in the upper left-hand side).

Make it easy

This exercise works particularly well on card as the tension remains taut. You can, of course, do it on fabric (as I have) but you may need to keep the final result in an embroidery frame to prevent the threads going slack.

"I cannot count my day complete 'til needle, thread and fabric meet". – Anon

IN THE LOOP: CHAIN AND BLANKET STITCHES

Fly, chain and blanket stitch are all classic embroidery stitches, made by forming loops that are stitched into place. Often used to depict flora and fauna, a meandering trail of stitches is perfect for suggesting lacy borders, plant tendrils or a fabulous tail of an exotic bird. Used densely, chain stitch is also an excellent filler stitch, while blanket stitch makes the ideal edging stitch.

EXPLORING BLANKET AND CHAIN STITCHES

Formed by looping thread around the needle, chain, fly and blanket stitch are perfect for adding surface decoration and texture to textiles. Once you have mastered the basic method for each, why not have a little fun and see what else can be done with these humble stitches?

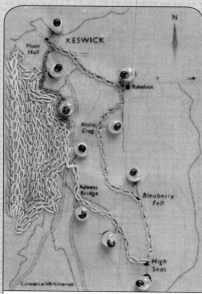

Mapping it out

A map was printed onto fabric with image transfer paper, then a favourite walk outlined with orange chain stitch. Points of interest along the way are highlighted with beads.

Blanket edging

After running stitch, blanket stitch is probably the next stitch a beginner might learn, yet its simplicity belies its versatility. As its name implies, it's the ideal stitch for edging fabric, or the pages of a book (see also pages 64–67).

Chain flowers

Chain stitch stems combined with seed beads and daisy stitch flowers would look sweet on a little girl's dress. I deliberately left some of the chains open to suggest tufts of grass.

Stitching on knitting

The simplest way to customise a plain piece of knitting is by adding chain stitch in between the columns of 'V's. This is particularly effective on details like pockets (see also pages 78–79).

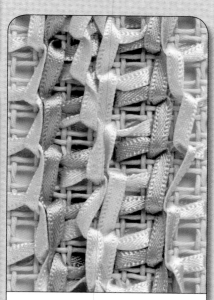

Ribbon embroidery

Several rows of blanket stitch made with ribbons on a tapestry canvas create an almost braid-like effect.

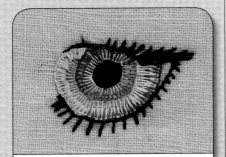

Stitching detail

Here, blanket stitch is used to depict an eye. Thicker thread was used for the eyelashes and pupil.

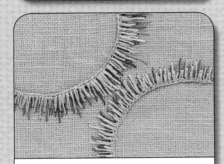

Long and short curves

Several curved rows of blanket stitch are worked on top of one another. I varied the stitch lengths to suggest thick, fluttering eyelashes.

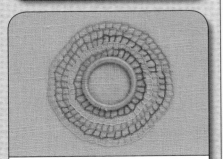

Couching down objects

A curtain ring was couched onto blue linen with thick orange cotton perlé thread, then a border of fine blanket stitches added around the ring.

Versatile blanket stitch

Blanket stitch has been used on this rustic-style decorative heart as an edging, and to couch a piece of suede string into place. It was then used as a filler stitch but I intentionally kept the spacing random and the spoke lengths uneven, to add to its rustic charm.

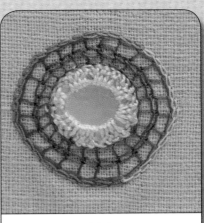

A little bit of *shisha*

Once the mirrored disc is fixed to the fabric, it is edged with buttonhole stitch. Blanket and buttonhole stitch are often confused, but they do differ. Blanket stitches are further apart while buttonhole stitches are more condensed, and instead of a simple loop, a little knot is formed when you move on to make a new stitch. I find the easiest way to remember the difference is that you work the point of the needle away from you for blanket stitch and towards you for buttonhole stitch (for *shisha*, see also pages 134–135).

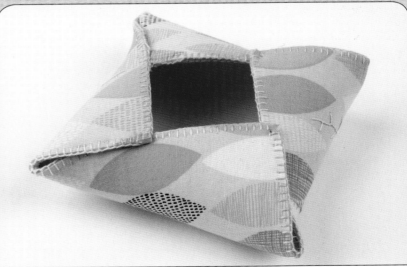

Creating three dimensions

Here, blanket stitch is used to strengthen the edges of a box made from a layer of fabric sandwiched onto craft foam. See page 154 for box construction.

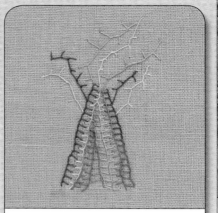

Blanket stitch bark

The bark of this tree is made up of blanket stitches; its branches are sewn in fly stitch.

Following the curve

Simple but effective: two types of ric-rac braid are couched onto fabric with wiggling blanket stitches.

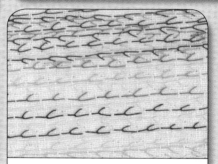

Simple stitches

A fly stitch flower.

Textural effects

Layers of overlapping fly stitch in different shades of a colour create a lovely surface texture.

Woven fly stitch

Try weaving a contrasting colour through rows of fly stitch.

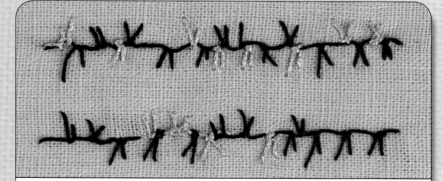

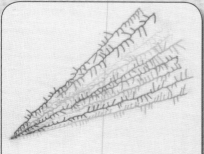

Up and down buttonhole stitch

Here, I kept changing the length and direction of my stitches. I created small barbs by working stitches very closely together (sometimes only a millimetre or so apart at their base). A combination of silver metallic and black thread was used for this barbed wire effect.

Vanishing stitches

Several rows of up and down blanket stitch were formed by constantly changing the direction of my stitches. The stitches decrease in size as they get nearer the vanishing point.

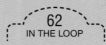

Dorset petals

Cover a curtain ring with blanket stitch in exactly the same way as you would for a Dorset button (see pages 100–101). Petals are formed by working rows of blanket stitches into the initial loops. Start a petal by making, for example, nine stitches, then work backwards along that row for seven stitches, back again for five stitches and so on until there is just one stitch left. Knot off the final stitch, weave in the ends, then make a new petal.

Creating fabric

I love creating fabric from thread and yarn, rather than merely using it to decorate, or hold fabric together. After adding a row of buttonhole stitches to a giant safety pin, I turned my work then added another row of stitches into the loops of the first. I continued to add further rows of stitching for several centimetres. Small tassels were added to complete the look. A similar treatment using super chunky yarn or rope and some driftwood would make a fabulous wall hanging!

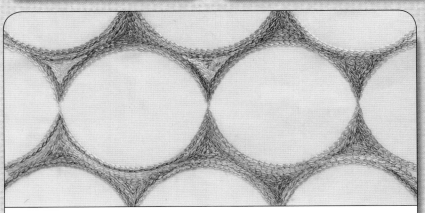

Filling with chain stitch

I used stranded satin floss for this chain stitch border.

Combining stitches

Leaf veins are depicted in fly stitch while the leaf's edge is drawn in chain stitch.

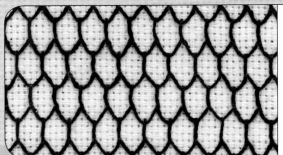

Honeycomb effect

Fly stitch is perfect for creating a honeycomb – just add bees.

You will need

Sewing guide, see page 156

Bookbinder's needle and thread of your choice: I used cotton perlé

Ruler and pencil

Paper for the pages

A heavier-weight card for the covers

Bone folder, or the curved side of a ruler will do

Awl

Bulldog clips

JAPANESE BOOKBINDING

If saddle-stitched notebooks are just a little too plain for your taste, perhaps Japanese bookbinding will appeal instead. The most notable feature is that the stitches wrap over the edges of the pages, which makes it ideal for using in conjunction with a blanket stitch detail along the turning edge of the front cover.

To make the book

1. Decide on the size of your book. Trim your inside papers to double the size of a single page, so that when they are folded in half, they will be the correct size. Trim your outer cover to just the tiniest fraction larger all round than the inside pages – literally 1mm (1/16in) or so will be enough!

2. With a soft, easily erasable pencil, mark out your sewing guides on the back cover (see page 156 for a guide, or create your own). For this type of binding, you want the first row of holes to be at least 5mm (1/4in) from the bound edge. If the holes are too close to the edge, the cover is more likely to tear after a little usage.

3. Fold the inside pages in half and sandwich them between the covers. Spend a little time getting everything even and perfectly aligned as any wobble will only get worse once you start to sew. When you're happy, clamp everything together with bulldog clips.

4. Pierce the holes through all layers with an awl, to make the sewing easier in the next steps. Try to pierce the holes vertically and not at an angle, otherwise the pages will become skewiff. This is probably the trickiest and most time-consuming bit, but it is worth being patient as your efforts will pay off in the end.

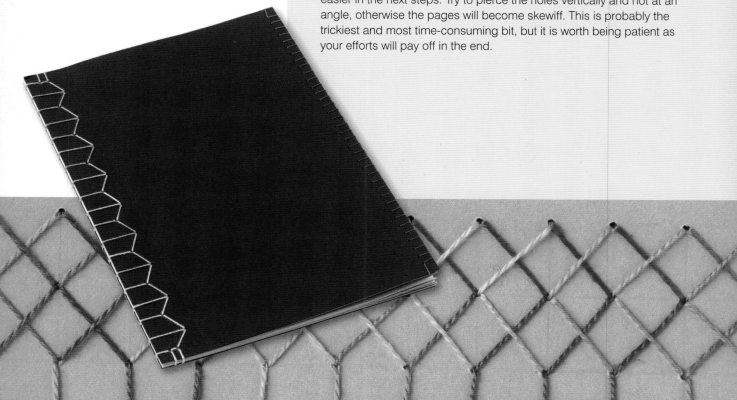

For the sewing

Thread a needle with a really long length of thread. I used ordinary cotton perlé. Starting at the back of the work (i.e. the back cover), bring your needle up through the back cover, through the pages and through hole 1. Don't knot the thread; just leave a long tail.

1: (refer to diagram 1) * take the thread over the spine and bring it back up through hole 1.

2: take the needle down through hole 2.

3: bring the needle up though hole 3 *.

4: (refer to diagram 2) repeat from * to *, stopping when you bring up the needle in hole 9.

5: take the thread over the top edge of the book and bring it up again through hole 9.

6: pass the needle down through hole 10, bring it over the top edge and back down again through hole 10.

7: carry the thread across the back of the work and bring it up through hole 9.

8: take it across and down through hole 11.

9: bring the thread over the top edge and back down through hole 11.

10: carry the thread across the back of the work and bring the needle up through hole 9.

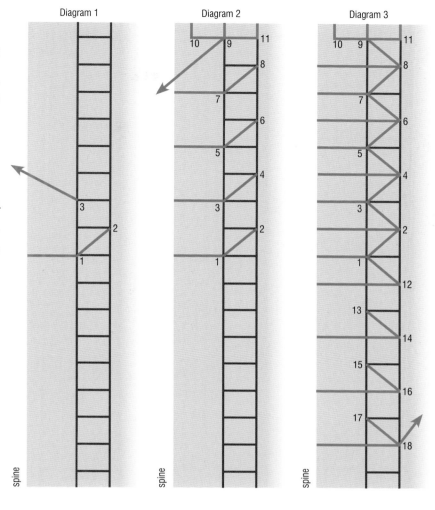

Diagram 1   Diagram 2   Diagram 3

spine   spine   spine

11: (refer to diagram 3) take the needle down through hole 8. Wrap the thread over the cover's spine, then take the needle down again through hole 8.

12: * bring up the needle through hole 7.

13: take the needle down through hole 6. Wrap the thread over the spine, then take the needle down again through hole 6.

14: bring the needle up through hole 5 *.

15: repeat from * to *, stopping when you have taken the thread down through hole 18 for the second time.

Continued overleaf...

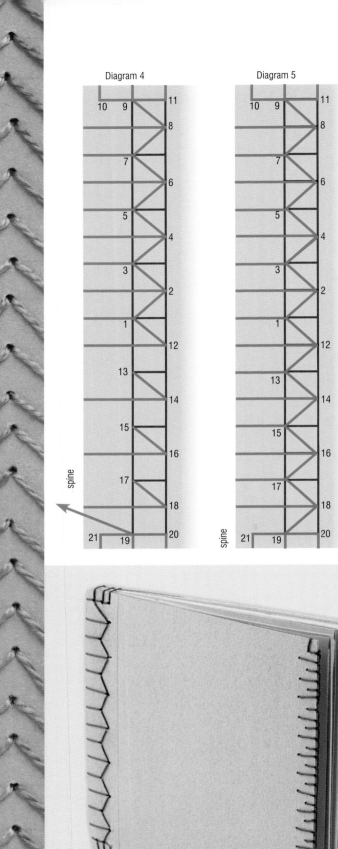

Diagram 4

Diagram 5

spine

16: (refer to diagram 4) bring the needle up through hole 19. Wrap the thread over the bottom edge and bring it up through hole 19 again.

17: take the thread across and down through hole 20. Wrap the thread from back to front and take down again through hole 20.

18: take the thread across the back of the work and bring the needle up through hole 19.

19: take the thread across and down through hole 21. Wrap the thread around the edge and take the needle down again through hole 21.

20: carry the needle across the back of the work and bring it up at point 19.

21: (refer to diagram 5) take the needle down through point 18, wrap the thread around the spine, from back to front, and pass the needle down to the back of work through hole 18.

22: * bring the needle up through hole 17. Take it down through hole 16.

23: wrap the thread around the spine of the book and take it back down through hole 16 *.

24: repeat from * to * until you work your way back to the very start of your work, ending with the thread at the back.

Knot off the loose ends, cut the excess and weave the remainder into your stitches.

Sketch and stitch

Try making another booklet to carry around with you that includes a combination of pages you can sew into and sketch onto. The assortment of pages might mean that the book doesn't look as neat as a purely paper counterpart, but it will be twice as useful.

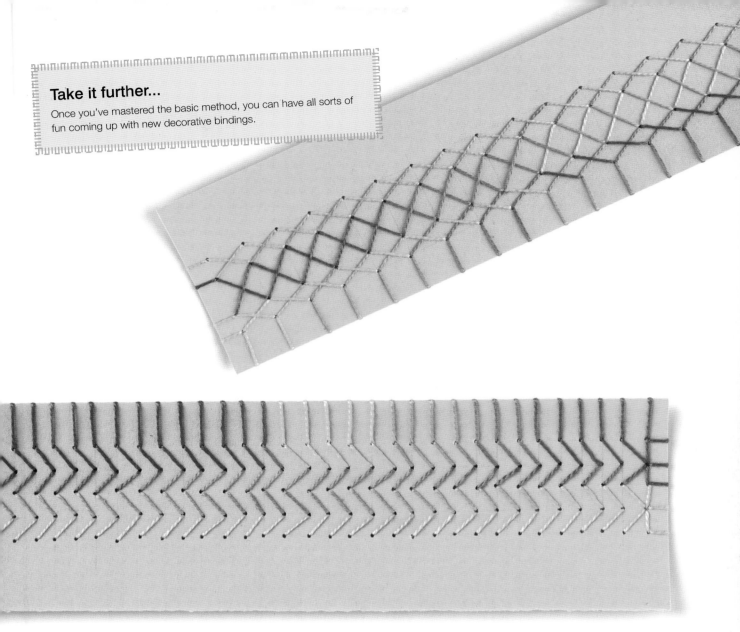

Take it further...

Once you've mastered the basic method, you can have all sorts of fun coming up with new decorative bindings.

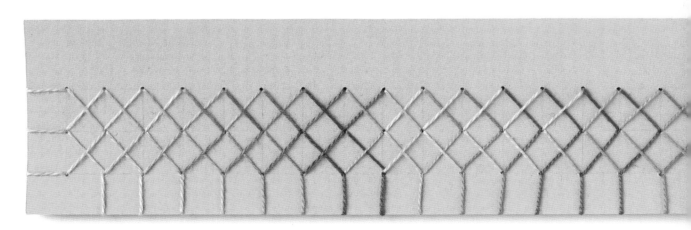

SAVING YOUR PENNIES

Once the epitomy of thrifty homemaking, penny mats have again become a popular craft. Due to their utilitarian nature, finding a complete antique penny mat is rare. A genuine example of this traditional American folk art will fetch large sums of money – certainly more than a few pennies.

During the American civil war (1861–1865) women saved scraps from army blankets, uniforms and old clothes. Then, using pennies as templates (American pennies were much larger then), circles were cut from the fabrics and sewn together with blanket stitching. Occasionally, pennies were left in the rugs to help them lie flat, and if an area became worn, more felt pennies were simply added to cover the holes. Old canvas, burlap or humble feed sacks were usually the backing of choice, as the mats had to be robust enough to withstand beatings and being regularly trampled upon.

As the fabric source was mainly military clothing or outerwear, colour schemes were dictated by what was available and tended to be sombre with just the occasional touch of something bolder, like red or blue. With age, antique examples have faded to beautifully subtle and muted tones.

Nowadays, colours can be anything but muted, while designs have become intricate or whimsical depending on the mat's intended use, which is likely to be decorative not utilitarian. Modern dyeing methods have vastly expanded the range of colours available, so penny mats now might include bright, cheerful pops of colour, with equally vibrant thread. Stitches aren't just limited to blanket stitch: my own penny mats often feature French knots, bullion stitch and chain stitch simply because I love the feel of sewing into felt and don't want to stop sewing once I've finished the blanket stitch edging (see examples shown right).

Neither are designs limited to circles – all manner of flora and fauna feature on modern penny mats – bunnies and chickens for Easter mats, pumpkins for Hallowe'en mats, even santas and elves for Christmas mats. You name it, anything goes! So much so, it may seem as if the only thing these mats have in common with the originals is that they are made from felt. Personally, I prefer the simplicity of the originals to the overworked complexity (and tweeness) of some – but by no means all – modern interpretations.

While the stitching is usually neater and more consistent on modern examples, this doesn't diminish the appeal of antique penny mats. Rather it adds to their charm, as the visible handiwork just affirms that these were items made with love by women who didn't have much, so used what was to hand to improve and make their homes more comfortable.

Here are a few penny mat-inspired samples that I made by layering up and embroidering circles of felt. See pages 70–71 for more information.

PENNY WALL HANGING

Nothing beats the feel of sewing into felt: it's so soft and forgiving that even the most naive of stitches looks beautiful against it. Any wonky stitches, so often seen on original penny mats, really don't matter here.

There's a whole lot more you can do with pennies than just make penny mats. Individual pennies make wonderful appliqués, especially on children's clothes, and are ideal for covering up small holes or stains that just won't budge. Enormous, brightly coloured pennies would look fabulous on a bedspead, or how about as decoration on a tent or wigwam? Or you could, as I've done, make use of some cashmere jumpers that were victims of a laundry disaster and create a wall hanging in muted tones of blue, pink and grey. For a finishing touch, embellish your hanging with some beachcombed pebbles that are both decorative and help the hanging hang straight. Whatever you decide to do, the best thing about pennies is that they are the perfect project to sew on the go; a few pennies, a needle and thread can fit in almost any purse.

"My soul is fed with needle and thread." – Anon

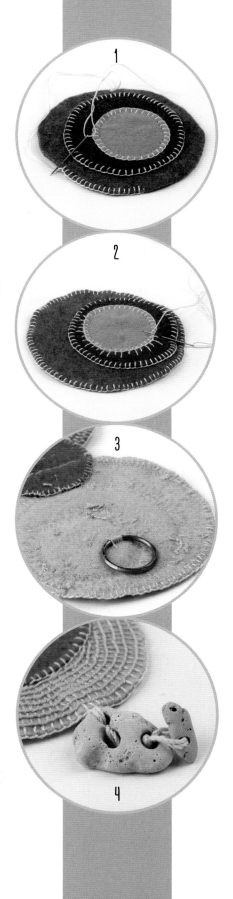

Tip

You could always add brightly coloured buttons or beads to the centre of your pennies.

Tip

For perfectly even stitches, mark a couple of lines on the thumb you hold your work with (not your sewing hand). Use them as a guide to space your stitches as you work.

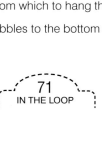

1. Start by stacking your pennies into groups of three – a large, a medium and a small – and stitch each group together with a tiny stab stitch placed at the centre of the smallest circle. Your circles don't have to be placed concentrically – as you can see, mine are extremely off-centre. Decorate the edge of each circle with blanket stitch, catching one layer to another as you sew.

2. As you add more stitches and join the layers together, the penny will start to feel less flimsy and create an irresistibly tactile texture. Sew as much, or as little, as you like. For these pennies I kept strictly to blanket stitch, using various weights and types of embroidery thread.

3. Add a blanket stitch edge to the four remaining small circles. Join the large pennies together by sewing the four small circles in between them. On the reverse of the top penny, I added a curtain ring from which to hang the piece.

4. Finally, I tied a couple of holey, beachcombed pebbles to the bottom of the hanging with some parcel string.

FLUXUS & MAIL ART

Fluxus was an *avant garde* art movement spanning the early 1960s to late 1970s. Like their predecessors, the Dadaists, the Fluxus movement sought to challenge the art establishment and its authority to decide what was and wasn't art, and how much it was worth.

Fluxus held that anyone could produce art, and that art shouldn't be reserved for the culturally elite or those 'in the know'. It actively encouraged audience participation and wanted to see art that was free from boundaries. As much as anything though, Fluxus embraced humour and didn't take itself too seriously.

Perhaps one of the most perfect expressions of Fluxus ideals is mail art – also known as 'correspondence art'. Mail art, as the name suggests, is art sent through the post, and by virtue of being sent by post it is able to reach a global audience, while being beyond the reach of the art cognoscenti. Mail art can also be a collaborative process, whereby the recipient adds their own artwork to the piece they've received, before sending it on to another person who might also add their own touches to the artwork. Naturally, the originator of the piece couldn't be precious about their work and had to embrace the collaborative process. There is no restriction regarding what media can be used: print, paint, collage, fabric, buttons and bits of string – all are perfectly acceptable.

So with this in mind, I decided to start off a piece of mail art, inspired by

a friend who has a liking for chunky-soled trainers. I started by mocking up a postcard and printed it onto iron-on transfer paper. Transfer paper is great if you want to print photographs on T-shirts, make wall hangings, or embellish a fancy dress costume, but it does feel very artificial, so I wouldn't recommend using it on everyday clothes – especially if the 'feel' of something is very important to you. Further, as transfer paper is quite brittle and prone to cracking and tearing if clamped in an embroidery frame, it's best to work without one, if you can.

Once the fabric cooled down, and the image was properly set, I added cream cotton perlé chain stitch to the midsole and decorated the eyelets with sparkly metallic buttonhole stitch. Then I sent the piece to a friend. Using a variety of green embroidery threads she added some blanket stitching, several whipped wheels and couched spokes that connect the wheels to each other. Since the piece has been returned to me, I've framed it with a shoe lace that I've embellished with chain stitch. So now it is ready to send on to someone else who can add their own touches…

Chain (stitched) letters: what might you send?

- Something personal like a map that locates all the recipients collaborating in the artwork?

- A family tree that could be passed on for parents to fill in each time there's a new addition to a branch of the family?

- A card that goes back and forth on the anniversary of a special event between family or friends?

- A crossword where each recipient fills in a clue?

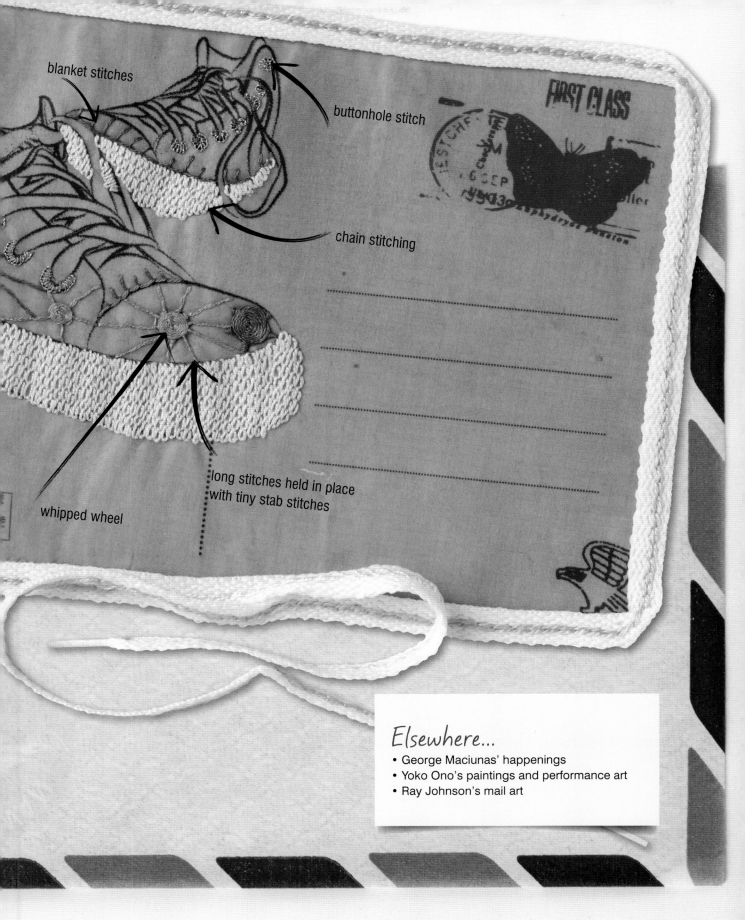

blanket stitches

buttonhole stitch

chain stitching

whipped wheel

long stitches held in place
with tiny stab stitches

FIRST CLASS

Elsewhere...
- George Maciunas' happenings
- Yoko Ono's paintings and performance art
- Ray Johnson's mail art

STITCHED MEMORIES

Do you like butter? Tell me the time? Can you make a garland? When we were young, it was possible to find the answer to these questions simply by picking a flower or two. To me, nothing brings back memories of childhood quite as much as meadow flowers and sycamore seeds (helicopters). To suggest the distance of memories, and how they can sometimes seem hazy, I've stitched into layers of sheer fabric.

How your piece will turn out depends on the memory you are trying to recapture. Perhaps you are trying to depict the thrill of your first ever bonfire party, in which case you might use dark muslins, velvets, metallic threads, some sequins and beads.

As I was trying to evoke a memory of a bright summer's day, I used the following

Semi-sheer fabrics including, silk, organza, muslin, and a piece of vintage cotton lawn that was once part of a child's dress, which I dyed with onion skins to get a delicate, papery yellow

Threads, including various weights of cotton perlé

Some white mohair knitting yarn

Cotton wool make-up remover pads

Water-soluble pen

Basic sewing kit

Elsewhere... Jo Beattie

For the buttercup

1. Draw the position of all your flowers onto the fabric with a water-soluble pen. Cut five circles from semi-sheer fabrics.

2. Arrange them into a flower shape and add a cluster of chain stitches for the stamens.

Tip
You don't have to use expensive fabrics like silk – tights are also semi-sheer, and come in a range of colours, so don't throw them away if they can be recycled.

For the dandelion

1. Collect together all the fabrics and threads, and check that you are happy with the colour mix.

2. Wind some mohair yarn into a loose circle and pin it to your fabric. Using a fairly thick cotton perlé thread, stitch it in place with 'dandelion' stitches (see page 151) – these are elongated fly stitches finished with a long chain stitch.

3. Cover your dandelion with a layer of semi-sheer fabric.

4. Add another coil of mohair yarn and, using a finer thread, add more dandelion stitches to the flower head. This time, make the stitches smaller and stagger their position. Tease apart a cotton pad until it is quite gauzy. Place the pad and a circle of loosely woven muslin over your stitching and pin in place.

5. With scissors and a needle, pick at the muslin, pull away some of the threads and let the cotton pad show through – try to create an interesting surface texture. Finally, stitch the muslin and cotton pad in place with a few very fine and randomly placed dandelion stitches.

When you think you have added enough layers, embroider into the top layer using a combination of daisy, sycamore (see page 151) and chain stitches. Let your stitches meander, and have fun!

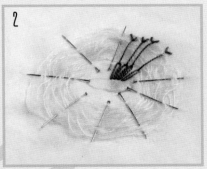

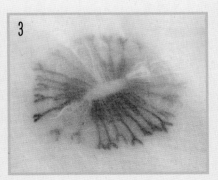

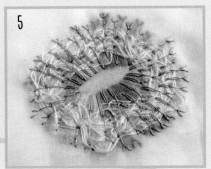

"Memory... is the diary that we all carry about with us."
– Oscar Wilde

SILHOUETTE—A—HULA

I was recently sifting through a selection of vintage posters and postcards. Among these treasures were hand-coloured photographs of Hula dancers and prints of Vargas pin-up girls, both of which inspired this piece of stitching.

I liked the idea of making my dancer a silhouette – albeit one with a few embellishments – but I needed an outline that was instantly recognisable, without any complicated details, or areas that could be misread and become confused. It was also important to streamline my shape as even the finest of stitches can make figures look bulkier than they are in reality.

It's all in the preparation

I started by making a little moodboard (1) that includes some pin-ups by the Peruvian painter, Alberto Vargas (1896–1982). His idealised depictions of the female form – like those of Jessica Rabbit™ and Barbie™ – teeter on the verge of being anatomically possible. Hands and feet are often unrealistically dainty, legs too long, while hips, waists and rib cages so compact, you wonder (if the pin-ups were to come to life) whether they really could accommodate vital organs.

From a stitching point of view, however, Vargas girls provide a perfect model to follow. So, taking my lead from Vargas, I exaggerated the curve and thrust of her hip, pinched in the waist, ankles and wrists and dramatically reduced the size of my dancer's hands and feet. Increasing the gap between my dancer's legs, and raising the point at which they touched, introduced a little more definition and meant they wouldn't look like a split tree trunk when stitched. As I intended for this to be a silhouette, it was also important to simplify the image. Elements such as facial features, clothing and wrist and ankle adornments are easy to read when drawn with traditional media, but unless you are working on an incredibly large scale, often dominate and become confusing when worked in stitch (2).

Once I was happy with the image, it was just a matter of transferring it to fabric, using a light box and a water-soluble pen (3).

Elsewhere...
• Jan Pieňkowski's silhouettes
• Alberto Vargas' pin-up girls

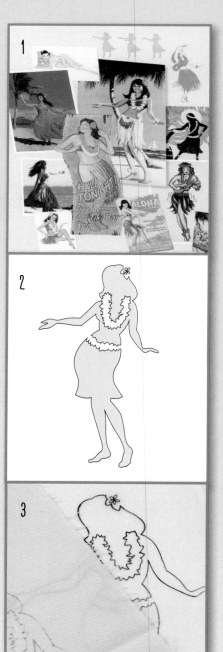

Now for the stitching

I stitched around the outline with isolated chain stitch (4, see page 149). Then I filled in the hula girl's body with further lines of chain stitch. Instead of knotting off the threads in the skirt, I left some tails long to suggest a real grass skirt (5). Using a few strands of alternative colour helps to give the grass skirt depth (see the finished piece). To make the garlands and flowers for my dancer's hair, I cut a few strips of organdie – you could use silk or organza. I ran a line of stitches down the centre of each strip, leaving a long tail of thread to use later (6). I then folded the organdie along the stitching line and snipped along the edges of fabric. Finally, I pulled the tail of thread so it bunched up the strip of organdie, and used the tail to sew the ruffle onto my dancer (7).

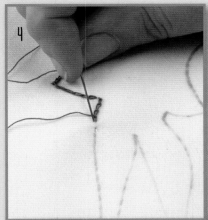

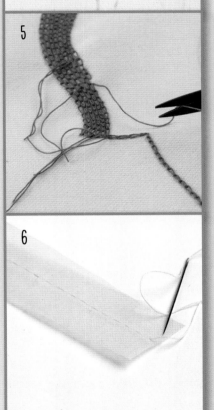

STITCHING ON KNITS

If you prefer one needle to two, or like the look of multi-coloured knits but have only just got the hang of stocking stitch, try these techniques for introducing colour to your knitted work the easy way.

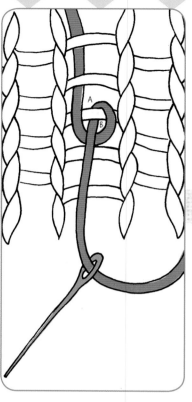

ADDING A CHAIN STITCH

The simplest way to get colour into a plain knit is to add chain stitch between the columns. If you're not a knitter, this might not mean much to you, so look closely at the front of a piece of plain knitting (stockinette). You will see that it is made up of columns of 'V's. If you stretch the fabric slightly, in between the 'V's you'll see little loops – these are the stitches that make up the reverse side of the knitting. Although you work from the right side of your knitting, it is the loops, or cross bars, on the back of the work, that you sew into.

To make the stitch

Thread a darning needle with yarn of the same thickness as the fabric you're sewing into. Starting at the back of the work (the loopy side), bring your needle through to the front of your work, exactly where you want your first stitch to start. Do not knot off the yarn at the back of the work; instead leave a tail, about 7.5cm (3in) in length, that you can weave into the loops when your work is complete. Bring the needle out at A. With the yarn under the needle, insert the needle back where you began. Take the needle under the cross bar, and bring it out at B. Pull the yarn snug to form a loop. Move on to the cross bar below to make the next stitch.

Single columns of chain stitch are effective on their own... but multi-coloured columns completely transform a plain knit into something really eye-catching.

ADDING DUPLICATE STITCH

Another way to add colour to knits is to use duplicate stitch or Swiss darning. Often used by knitters to mimic or correct errors in Fairisle knitting, duplicate stitch is ideal if you want to add decorative details to knitwear without having to juggle lots of yarns at the same time.

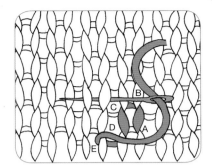

To make the stitch

Starting from the back of your work, and leaving a long tail to weave in later, bring your needle out at A. Insert the needle at B (so you cover the forward-slanting stroke of the 'V') and carry it across the back of the work to C, then over the backward-slanting stroke of the 'V' and in at D, ready to carry across to E, to start all over again. You are literally covering the 'V's with another colour, which is why the yarn you use for sewing should be the same weight used for knitting.

ADAPTING A CROSS-STITCH CHART

Any cross-stitch chart can be used as a Swiss darning pattern. The examples of cross stitch and duplicate stitch shown below have been worked from the same chart (shown below right).

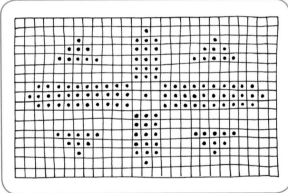

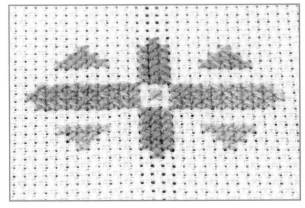

Tip

Useful as well as decorative, Swiss darning is a handy technique to employ when it comes to saving worn out knits from the bin. If you want to mend a moth hole or patch a worn area (such as an elbow or the heel of a sock) simply darn as shown above but start several stitches before the weakened area begins. Work across the weakened area, then continue for a few more stitches. Repeat until the worn area has been reinforced.

"A gentle heart is tied with an easy thread." – George Herbert

TEXTURE: RAISED STITCHES

French knots, bullion stitches and whipped wheels are perfect for adding a warm, semi-relief texture to work. Combine them with other embroidery stitches to create elaborate designs and realistic imagery, or concentrate on a single raised stitch, repeated many times, for a more abstract effect.

EXPLORING RAISED STITCHES

Knots, bullions and wheels take on a life of their own that sometimes seems independent of the fabric on which they are worked. Clusters of knots might suggest a bouclé effect, while deliberately leaving long tails on knots creates fringing that moves when your hand brushes against its edge. Whipped wheels can appear as if they are growing on a background, and when worked on a hoop or ring, rather than fabric, look equally intriguing viewed from either side.

French knot texture

Creating knots of differing sizes, using various types of thread, is great practice for perfecting your French knots technique.

Double-sided tufts

Lengths of jute string have been sewn and knotted into both sides of tapestry canvas. On one side, the tails have been unravelled and trimmed to create soft tufts. I then flipped the canvas and sewed into the other side, leaving the tails untrimmed and dangling. The result is an interesting combination of knots and tufts or tails on both sides of the canvas – a technique that would lend itself well to a wall hanging.

Mesh fringing

A piece of reinforced woven plastic mesh provides a grid to work variegated cotton threads into. The tails have been left deliberately long and the result is a double-sided swatch.

French knot and fringe

Curving rows of silky French knots were topped with long-tailed knots to create this shiny caterpillar.

Scattered knot stitches

I wanted to suggest beads spilling onto a background, so tiny French knots were the obvious stitch. They are worked more densely at the centre, then sparsely and in lighter colours towards the edges of the scatter.

Drawing with stitch

This swatch is based on a Charles Rennie Mackintosh drawing of a tree, with the knots serving to hold the 'branches' of the tree in place.

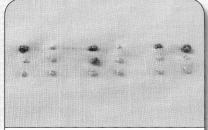

Braille in stitch

The raised texture of French knots makes them ideal for conveying messages in languages such as braille...

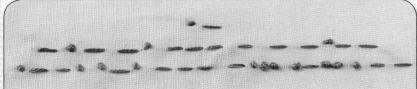

Morse code in stitch

Can you work out what this one says? (See below for the solution.)

Embellishing prints

I'm not usually a lover of prints: screen-printed surfaces always look a little flat to me. Bold and lively prints like this one, however, are a different kettle of fish. Picking out details such as rows of dots and embellishing them with French knots gives the fabric more depth and texture.

Creating texture

Here, French knots are used to hold pinched fabric in place.

Morse code in stitch
Solution: A KNOTTY PROBLEM

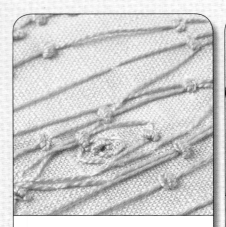

Bullion couching

Like the drawing with stitch sample on page 83, a similar effect is achieved by couching the 'branches' in place with bullion stitches.

Couching leather cord

A knotted leather cord – used in jewellery making – is couched in place with bullion stitches. I used a contrasting thread for a bold effect.

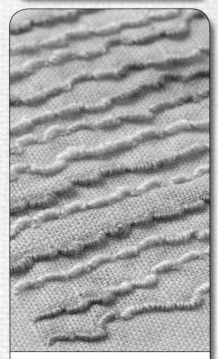

Bullion bugs

These bullion bugs are made from fluorescent acrylic thread. The black felt background makes them really stand out and is easy to sew into, meaning that the thread is less likely to snag and get tangled – some knots are less welcome than others!

Felted fish

I felted a 'stone' shape and stitched a piece of tumbled sea glass into the felt. Beads and bullion stitches were then added to create this very strange 'fish'.

Rows of bullion

Experiment with bullion stitch and variegated thread to create graduated rows of texture and colour.

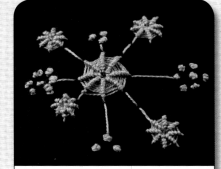

Starburst

Whipped wheels, long stitches and French knots in metallic thread on felt are a great combination for suggesting a starburst in the night sky.

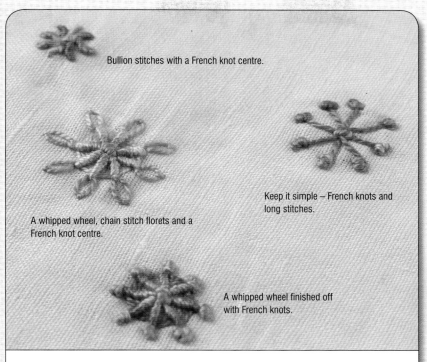

Bullion stitches with a French knot centre.

A whipped wheel, chain stitch florets and a French knot centre.

Keep it simple – French knots and long stitches.

A whipped wheel finished off with French knots.

Raised stitch flowers

Raised stitches are the embroiderer's perennial favourite when it comes to sewing flowers. Try one of these examples or experiment to create your own.

Oyster wheel

Whipped wheels always remind me of the limpets and barnacles you find around rock pools at the beach, so it seemed natural to sew one around this oyster shell.

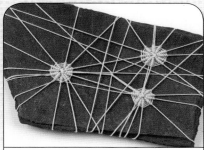

Whipped slate

A piece of slate wrapped with thread and decorated with whipped wheels creates a cobweb effect so would make a perfect Hallowe'en coaster or placemat for a dinner party.

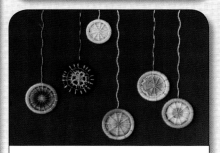

Whipped buttons

Dorset buttons are basically whipped wheels worked around a ring...

Play time

Never be afraid to experiment... Even if a swatch doesn't lead to a fully fledged project you won't have wasted your time. Here, I've stitched wheels onto layers of net and an unravelled bathroom puff to see what effect might be achieved. I deliberately distressed the layers by holding areas over a candle so they melted together. The result? I can see this working well on a Hallowe'en costume, or for a Miss Havisham bridal dress!

Guitar string wheel

Here I embellished a guitar string with glass beads and nylon beading thread, and played around with the principle of a whipped wheel, randomly working backwards and forwards to create this abstract cobweb.

MINI QUILT

A quilt doesn't have to be complicated to be eye-catching. Fancy free-motion embroidery and intricate English paper piecing can look amazing but take time and practice to get right. So why not try hand-tying? Hand-tying a quilt is often dismissed as a beginner's technique, or only suited to baby quilts, but I believe hand-tied quilts have a charm all of their own that will appeal to a modern rustic sensibility. This lap quilt is made from half-square triangles in a range of denims, linens and indigo-dyed cottons. Making half-square triangles couldn't be simpler…

You will need

Fabric: enough for your patchwork top plus a larger piece – large enough to back the quilt, with an additional 4cm (1½in) all round to serve as a binding

Wadding/batting: a piece measuring the same size as your patchwork

Needle

Linen thread, or medium thickness cotton perlé

Fabric spray glue

Quilters' ruler

Rotary cutter

Basic sewing kit

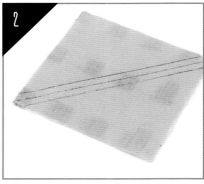

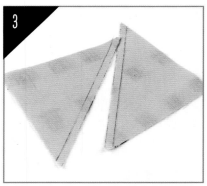

Making your half-square triangles

1. Start by cutting your fabric into squares. Mine were 13cm (5in) squares which, by the time the patchwork was complete, meant that each square measured 11.5 x 11.5cm (4¼ x 4¼in).

2. Pair up your squares: perhaps pair a patterned square with a plain square, or choose pairs of contrasting colours. On the wrong side of one of them, draw a diagonal line from one corner to the other. Draw two further lines, 5mm (¼in) either side of the first line.

3. Pin your fabric squares right sides together, ensuring they are properly aligned, since even a hint of wonkiness will really show on the finished patchwork. Sew along the two outer lines using a fairly short stitch length. You don't need to reverse for a few stitches at the ends of rows, as by the time the patchwork is complete you will have gone over the seam ends so they should be quite secure.

4. Using a rotary cutter and quilters' rule, cut along the unsewn central line. You should now have two triangles which, when opened and pressed flat, are a perfectly seamed combination of two different fabrics. Cut off the little dog ears of fabric to complete.

Arranging your half-square triangles (HSTs)

1. When your HSTs are complete, arrange them into a pleasing design – mine is shown right. Using a 5mm (¼in) seam allowance, sew the HSTs together. Be systematic: first sew the individual rows, then join these together in pairs until all rows are assembled. When you sew the rows together, don't just start at one end and put your foot to the pedal, as any inaccuracies will only worsen by the time you've finished. Instead, start at the middle of a row and join a couple of squares to the right of the centre, then a couple to the left of the centre and so on. That way you can even out any discrepancies as you go.

2. Now sandwich your top, wadding/batting and backing together. You can tack/baste the layers together, but fabric spray is so much easier – and quicker! Make the binding from the excess backing by turning in 2cm (¾in) of the border to form a hem. Then fold the border over again (so the hem is hidden) and bring it to the front of the work. Tuck in any ends and sew everything in place.

Tip

Rather than trying to match your thread to one of the fabrics in your patchwork only to find it clashes, or stands out too brightly, try using grey thread. Somehow it magically blends in with virtually all fabrics!

Why quilt?

There are three main reasons. First, quilting holds the layers together; second, it's decorative; and third, quilting adds to the insulatory properties of a quilt. Hand-tying might not score highly on the third point, but it certainly does on the other two.

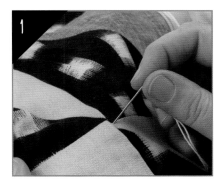

Making the knots

Making the knots is child's play. Thread a needle with something substantial – linen thread or thick cotton perlé are ideal. Work with the thread doubled but don't tie a knot at the ends.

1. Insert your needle in the front of your work, right where you want the knot to be. Leave a 5cm (2in) tail on the fabric surface.

2. Move the needle along by 5mm (¼in) and bring it to the front of your work. Cut another 5cm (2in) tail and simply tie the tails together with a double knot. Trim or don't trim the tails according to preference.

DRAWING WITH STITCH

Elsewhere...
- **The drawings of Charles Rennie Mackintosh**
- **Paul Klee's etchings**
- **The textile art of Paddy Killer**

I have always felt that drawing and sewing have much in common; that they are equally valid languages that can be used to describe the world around us. Recently, while visiting a gallery in Skibbereen (Cork, Ireland), a pen and ink line drawing of what looked like tailors' tacks caught my attention.

The more I looked at the rest of the work on display, the more convinced I became that the artist – Jim Wilson – must have an affinity for stitching. It turns out that as well as a love of Oriental and Islamic pattern, the greatest influence on Jim's work was indeed the intricate stitching of his seamstress mother! Stitch can be used to realistically represent the world, but as thread tends not to blend as well as pencil or paint, the viewer has to stand some distance away before all the individual stitches blur into a cohesive whole. When you do that, you lose sight of the texture, and that surely is the unique beauty of textile art?

To avoid a naive effect where the result just looks as if it has been poorly observed, I believe that stitching works best at capturing the spirit of a subject when used in a stylised or abstract way. Abstraction is key to Jim's work too, as is the repetition of deceptively simple marks to create a complex-looking whole. Jim uses this technique to convey messages, such as the effect of deforestation on the environment, as he does in the piece shown above right, entitled *Logging*, which depicts piles of cut timber awaiting collection.

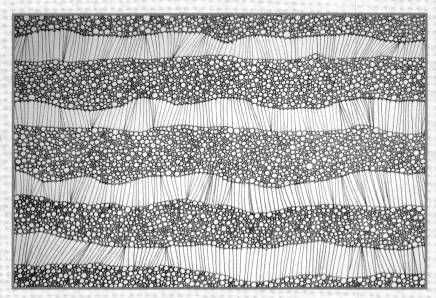

Painting with a needle

Even the most exacting schools of sewing recognise the importance of stylising a subject to make it easier to read when drawn in stitch. A look at work produced by The Royal School of Needlework illustrates how deliberately flattening, or simplifying, an image can result in a far more pleasing surface pattern and texture than fruitlessly trying to mimic real life could ever achieve. A notable exception however, is silk shading (also known as 'painting with a needle'). By replicating the subtle tonal changes in a subject (often a fruit, flower, plant or animal), a combination of long and short stitches blend together to produce a highly natural-looking object.

"Drawing [sewing] is taking a line [thread] for a walk." – Paul Klee

In the stitched sample right, *Seaweed on Shifting Sands*, I wanted to make an impact using only a single stitch, repeated many times. On quilters' linen, I used my trusty water-soluble pen to draw the curves of sand and filled them in with tight clusters of tiny French knots in variegated cotton perlé. To suggest the tide's direction, and the shadow side of the sands, I made sure to always fill the curves in from the same direction. I also added more knots where the curves are deepest. Then, I used a lighter row of French knots and irregular lengths of very fine cotton thread knotted in place on the underside of the curves to create a fringe, or seaweed-like, effect.

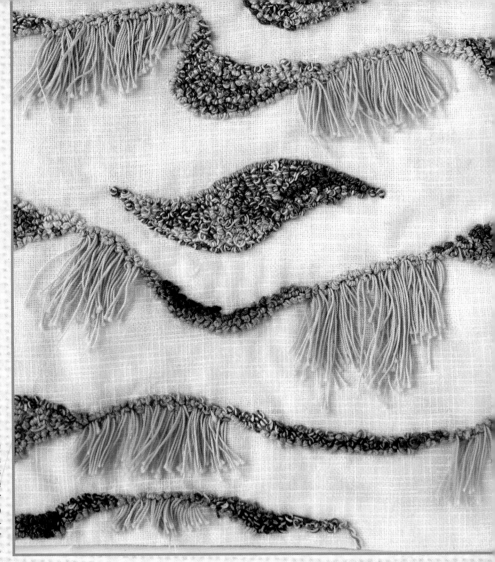

Stylisation doesn't have to mean complete abstraction. Textile artist Jo Beattie uses a combination of illustrative and sewing techniques to represent the human figure and the importance of memory. In the piece shown below from her *Precious Memories* series, stitch is used to reproduce clothing – its patterns and colours – something Jo believes is inextricably linked to our recollection of those we have known and loved.

DREAMTIME LIZARD

Dreamtime art plays a vital role in keeping Aboriginal culture alive and its stories provide a structure for how society should be run. It tells of the spirit ancestors, who created the world and everything in it and ordained the Aborigines' place within the world. Symbols used in Dreamtime art can have multiple meanings, depending on their context, and often feature totemic animals such as snakes, which can represent the cycle of life, or lizards, which might symbolise the dream world and looking to the future.

When drawn, snakes and lizards are usually depicted as if looked at from above. This graphic representation makes them ideal for using on textiles, where you want a simple motif and a bold splash of colour. Before painting my lizard on fabric, I played around with inks and bleach on a few scraps of cloth. Because of the subject matter, I wanted the colours to look quite 'earthy' but there's no reason why you couldn't use brighter colours.

You will need

Some robust cloth

Template (see page 153)

Indian ink

Fabric pens

Coloured inks

Chunky marker pens

Bleach

Cotton buds

Old paintbrushes or toothbrushes – anything not too precious that can be used for applying paint and bleach

Needle and threads

Water-soluble pen

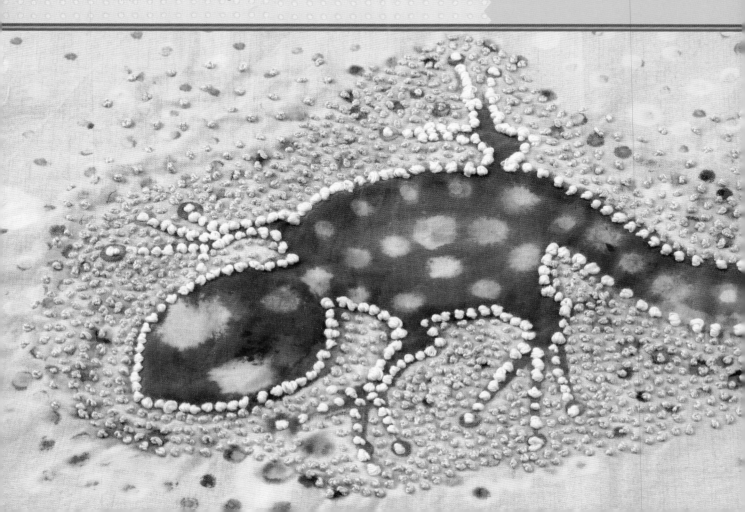

1. Once I had experimented and was confident about using the bleach and paint, I transferred a lizard shape to the fabric using a lightbox and water-soluble pen (see page 153 for the template). Because I knew the fabric would take quite a battering, I used something thick and strong.

2. I filled in the body with a deep magenta, then, while the ink was still wet, touched up the outer edges with a darker red and allowed the colours to bleed into each other.

3. Using a cotton bud dipped in bleach, I made big dots on the lizard. With another bud dipped in ink I added borders of dots around the lizard's outline. Some were overlaid with bleach, others left as they were.

4. Now for the stitching. Only French knots were used to decorate this lizard, as I thought them best for representing the dots so typically seen in Dreamtime art. First I outlined the lizard using *sashiko* cotton thread – wrapping the thread around my needle two or three times to get super chunky knots.

5. The background is decorated with smaller French knots, this time made using a finer cotton perlé thread. As you can see, there are quite a lot of them, so if you decide to do your own Dreamtime textile, you'll soon become an expert at French knots.

Experimenting with ink and bleach

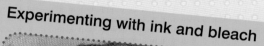

Tortoiseshell effects are achieved by splattering bleach over Indian ink, then, using a cotton bud dipped in ink, adding dots to some of the bleached out areas.

These flowers are made by placing a large, round-headed brush, loaded with lots of red ink, flat on the fabric, and not worrying about how much the colour runs. While still wet, I dropped a bit of black Indian ink into the centre of the petals, and then a drop of bleach, and let serendipity take effect.

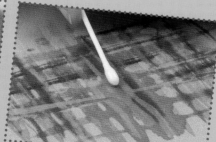

A tartan effect was created using horizontal and vertical lines of colour with dabs of bleach dropped on to them.

"Those who lose dreaming are lost." – Aboriginal proverb

SEAMLESS REPETITION

If you like repeat patterns but shy away from trying out your own because you think they involve unfathomable and complicated design processes, think again. They are actually devilishly simple to produce, and since repeat patterns have long been associated with textiles, it's well worth knowing how to produce them.

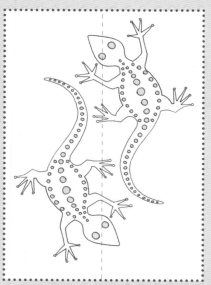

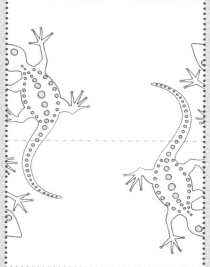

1. Choose your image: I'm using my Dreamtime lizard from pages 90–91 (see page 153 for template). Either set up an A4 (21 x 30cm/ 8¼ x 11¾in) document in a software program of your choice and position your image centrally on the page, or draw the design onto paper. Play around: flip and repeat the image until you get a pleasing design. It is important that none of the artwork touches the paper's edge. Slice the design vertically down the centre of the image, as indicated by the red dashes.

2. Slide the left-hand side of the image over to the right-hand side of the page, and the right-hand side of the image to the left-hand side of the page. Group the images in your software program – or tape the paper pieces together if using the traditional method – so that they don't accidentally move around, then slice the image in half horizontally across its centre.

3. Slide the bottom half of the image to the top of the page, and the top half of the image to the bottom of the page. Again, group or tape the pieces so they don't lose their position.

Elsewhere...

M. C. Escher's interlocking lizards and any of William Morris's repeat patterns

4. Fill in any central areas with other design elements… more lizards, more dots; just don't let any new additions touch the edges of the paper!

One lonely Dreamtime lizard is transformed into a whole loungeful of lizards.

Tip

For the traditionalists: don't let a lack of technology put you off – William Morris managed to produce stunning repeat patterns without the aid of a computer. Exactly the same results can be achieved using paper, a craft knife and some tape. If possible, make copies of each stage (either a tracing or photocopy) as your work will become quite fragile the more you cut and tape it together.

5. Finally, tile the design as many times as you like. There's no need to overlap the edges – just butt them together for a seamless repetition.

TALKING KNOTS

Knots are an integral part of textiles: lace making, knitting and macramé all depend on the manipulation of them. We use knots to anchor a line of sewing and stop it slipping away, and decoratively as French knots or bullion stitches to add texture to a piece of sewing.

But it isn't just crafters who use knots – any sailor worth their salt should be able to tie at least a handful of knots, while superstitious people sometimes tie knots in handkerchiefs as a reminder of something important they need to do. But surely an entire ancient empire basing its accounting system on knots is the ultimate expression of knot appreciation?

For the Incas, knots were a reliable system that perfectly overcame a lack of a writing system as we might recognise one. Instead of written Arabic numbers, the Incas used brightly coloured ropes with a series of knots on each strand to record everything from taxes and stock numbers to census information. These ropes were called quipus – there might have been as many as 2000 individual quipus held on what looked like a necklace but which was in fact an ingenious accounts ledger. Quipus used a base ten counting system, and a strand representing, say 752 items, might look something like the knotted rope shown on the facing page. Much larger numbers (in the thousands) might have a knot that represented a number to the power of ten.

Quipus were an extremely successful method of keeping accounts and their demise was only due to the Spanish colonisation of South America. The Spanish sought to convert the South Americans to Catholicism, and anything to do with the culture or beliefs of indigenous inhabitants was seen as idolatrous and anti-Catholic and therefore wiped out. This included the Incan accounting system – the result of which is that very few quipus remain in existence.

A quipu-inspired textile

While I'm happy to stick with a calculator for my accounts, I was keen to incorporate some of the features of quipus into this sample. The materials I've used are very basic: some household string, a piece of quilters' linen and some cotton perlé. Firstly, I cut my string into various lengths and knotted them, sometimes leaving a long gap between the clusters of knots, sometimes evenly spacing them out. Then I couched them onto the linen with bullion stitch and finally added plain running stitch to the background.

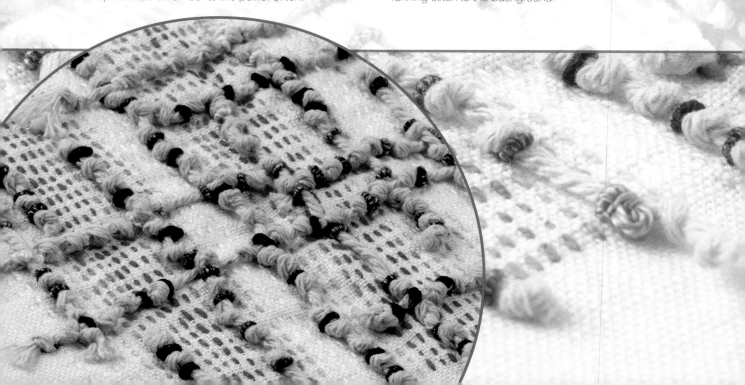

Removing and preventing knots

Knots can be a cause of frustration when thread tangles or twists back on itself and threatens to ruin your stitches. Here are some tips for avoiding and unravelling them.

1. As you sew, your thread inevitably gets twisted. Every so often, let go of your needle and let it dangle – do this over a table or hard surface where your needle will be easily visible if you think you might lose it – the thread should spin itself straight.

2. Untwisted thread should hang in a 'U' shape from work to needle – twisted thread looks like a lasso. If your thread is lassoing, twist your needle in the opposite direction as you sew. Get into the habit of twisting your needle in the opposite direction as you work to prevent threads tangling in the first place.

3. If thread starts to snarl up mid-stitch, don't yank it through the fabric – this will almost certainly cause a knot. Instead, stop, pull the tangle towards you so it unravels, then gently pull the thread through from the other side using your fingers. I find it helps to insert my needle in the loop to give the thread something to feed itself around smoothly. When you've done this, untwist the thread as explained above.

4. If you get what looks like a loop with a knot at its base, insert your needle in the loop and gently pull it away from the fabric. The knot should slide towards the needle. When it has done so, remove your needle, take hold of the thread either side of the knot (which is actually just a small twist) and give a little tug – the knot should magically disappear.

5. Using shorter lengths of thread means there's less to get tangled in the first place.

6. Run your thread through beeswax or thread conditioner before you start stitching – this will help to keep the thread slick and silky.

Here you can see that each coloured section represents a different type of number: hundreds, tens and single digits. This sample would represent 752: seven hundreds, five tens and then two.

Elsewhere...
See the work of weaver Anni Albers, who travelled in South America and was an admirer of its textile traditions, including quipus, and the use of visual language

NAUTICAL KNOTS

Have you ever wondered what a nautical knot is and if the use of the word 'knot' actually relates to knots as we know them? Well it isn't a coincidence: until the mid-19th century, a ship's speed was measured by tying a length of rope with knots evenly spaced at a distance of eight fathoms (14.4m/47ft 3in) along it to a specially weighted board. This board, which was able to remain upright in the water and resist its pressure, was then cast into the water and reeled out. As the knots passed between the hands of one sailor, another counted the speed at which they did so with a 30-second sand glass. This enabled sailors to calculate how many 'knots' they were travelling per hour and estimate journey times.

NATURAL DYES

When I first got into sewing, I was a sucker for the latest fabric ranges and built up quite a stash of designer prints, many of which now languish in a drawer, never having encountered scissors, needle or thread. I suspect I'm not alone in this tendency of sewers (especially novices) to hoard, but the trouble with buying the latest thing is that everyone else has it too.

Dyeing fabrics is a great way to personalise them. For example, indigo dyeing using *shibori* techniques can look stunning and is certainly worth trying – if you have the space (see pages 104–105). If not, try to enrol on a course or workshop – it will be money well spent. But what if there are no available courses or workshops, and the people you live with don't take kindly to the mess and inconvenience of negotiating their way around vats of dye, or you hogging the sink and then hanging damp fabric all over a shared space?

Rust dyeing

Thankfully it is possible to dye fabric on a small scale without the need for specialist equipment. One of my favourite methods is rust dyeing, which produces lovely results. First, 'scour' or rinse your fabric in water to rid it of any impurities such as starch. Then fold, wrap, sew or twist your fabric around bits of metal and put them in a bowl filled 50/50 with water and vinegar (1). I used rosé wine vinegar for this piece, but other acetic acids such as lemon juice or regular vinegar produce similar results. After an hour or so, remove the fabric from the bowl and leave it in the air to dry, and wait for the oxidisation process to work its magic. Once unwrapped, you can see the *shibori* effect in all its glory; both from the stain left by the rusted screw and the delicate lines of the thread that held it in place (2).

1

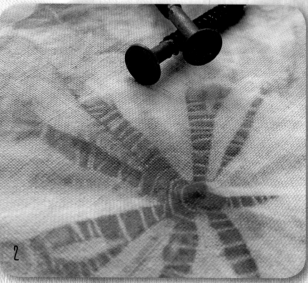

2

Mushroom printing

If rust dyeing is still too messy for you, why not try mushroom printing? All you need is fabric and mushrooms – that's it! Remove the stalk and any ragged bits from the edges of the cup that might prevent the underside making contact with the fabric. Simply leave the mushroom to rest on the fabric (3). When the mushroom has dried out, remove it and you'll be left with an impression of its underside (4). Try the technique out on different fabrics to see which looks best. As this is a technique that might not withstand laundering, iron your prints to help set them.

I was so pleased with my print that I decided to embellish it with stitch. I added bullion stitches to suggest the frilled cup edge, long stitches for some of the gills (lamellae) on its underside and French knots for the centre and surrounding spores (5).

And one more thing

I also keep a large, lidded pan and wooden spoon to one side that I use especially for dyeing small amounts of fabric. I scour the fabric before dyeing it but usually add a mordant, such as alum powder (plus some cream of tartar) to help fix the colours. In the past, I've had some fabulous results using onion skins, which produced a greenish tinge, and avocado skins, which produced a beautiful dusty rose colour.

Elsewhere...
For more on natural dyeing, see the work of India Flint

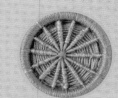

THE RISE AND FALL OF BUTTONY

In England during the 18th to mid-19th centuries, hundreds of thousands of Dorset buttons were produced each year. Entire communities were involved in their production – including prisoners and orphans – such was the demand for Dorset buttons.

The production of Dorset buttons was a cottage industry that helped supplement the incomes of the poor. Farm labourers, whose work was seasonal, widows with no other form of income, and women who had to look after children could all earn money by working from home. When their work was complete, outworkers delivered their batches to button depots, such as the one owned by Blandford-based draper Robert Fisher, who then distributed the buttons to travelling merchants. It was a system that worked well for all: no factory overheads for the distributors, and a reliable income for the makers who could earn up to two shillings for making as many as six to seven dozen buttons per day!

Originally, Dorset buttons were formed around a cross-section of horn from the Dorset sheep (earlier versions called high tops, or knobs, were worked over a rolled-up scrap of fabric), but later buttons used other materials for a mould, and varied depending on the occupation of the maker. A blacksmith, for example, might use a piece of metal, a leatherworker, a piece of leather; scraps of twisted cloth were also popular moulds for button-making. The thread used to cover the mould could also vary – the Blandford cartwheel button (a variant of the Dorset Button) used lace thread left over by the Huguenots, who had worked in the area until the decline of its lace-making industry.

Although cloth buttons had been made for centuries (Charles I reportedly went to his execution wearing a waistcoat fastened with them), it was thanks to Abraham

Case that the Dorset button industry flourished. It has been said that during his time as a soldier in northern Europe, Abraham noticed how soldiers would replace missing buttons by twisting a piece of fabric over a form, then fastening it to their uniforms with a length of thread. This, and exposure to the wealth of lace in Belgium, may well have inspired Abraham's interest in needlelace buttons.

Eventually Abraham set up an import–export business for needlelace buttons in Shaftesbury, Dorset that was to prove so successful it earned the county its nickname, *Buttony*. However, it was his grandson Peter who introduced the greatest development in the production of Dorset buttons. In keeping with the spirit of the industrial revolution, Peter helped develop a rust-free metal alloy ring, which he gave to outworkers to use as a button mould. Naturally, this extended the life of the buttons and meant they wouldn't rust after washing or exposure to weather.

Although it was already in decline, it was another triumph of the industrial revolution and advances in mass production methods that sounded the death knell for Buttony. At the Great exhibition of 1851, John Ashton introduced his button-making machine. Requiring very little skill to operate, and able to produce buttons at a rate even the fastest of workers could never hope to compete with, Ashton's machine virtually wiped out the Dorset button industry. As a result, many were left starving and penniless – their only hope for survival, to make a new life in America.

MAKING BUTTONS

Elsewhere...
Look at Pinterest for Dorset button inspiration

Dorset buttons are easy to make, but be warned, making them can become an obsession – I should know – I have a large jar full of them on my shelf! The most well known is the crosswheel, or cartwheel, which is a flat button worked around a ring. Earlier versions, called Dorset knobs, or high tops, were often as high as they were wide.

MAKE A DORSET CROSSWHEEL

To make one, you will need

Curtain ring

Thread (such as cotton perlé)

Tapestry needle

1. Start by 'casting' the ring – this is when you cover it with blanket stitch. Make sure you have enough thread on your needle to complete the casting and the 'laying', and preferably the 'rounding' too: 91.5cm (36in) should be enough.

2. Slick the edges by turning the ridges to the back of the ring so they can't be seen.

3. Wrap the thread around the ring – this is known as laying (3a). The number of times is up to you but you need to end up with an even number of spokes (3b). When you've done this, secure the spokes with a little cross at their centre (3c). This is the time to ensure the cross is properly centred and all spokes evenly spaced, as you won't be able adjust them once you start rounding. If you think you might run out of thread before you finish the button, join in a new piece now before you start the next step.

4. Now you move on to the rounding stage. Bring your needle up from the back of your wheel and backstitch over one spoke. Your needle will now be at the back of the wheel, so move on to the next spoke, and once again, backstitch over it. Keep repeating this until you have filled the wheel; to help me remember the sequence, I often think of this as two steps forward, one step back!

5. Finally, cast off by taking the needle to the back of the work, secure with a couple of discreet stitches and either cut off the tail, or use it as a shank to attach to something else.

Once you've mastered this technique, why not try your hand at the Dorset basket? This is where you alternate the spokes you backstitch over on each round.

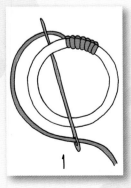
1

3a

3b

3c

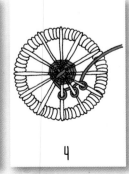
4

MAKE A DORSET KNOB

1. Run a line of neat little running stitches around the edge of the circle and pull the thread. Stuff the cavity with wadding/batting, then pull the thread tightly and secure with a few stitches. This will be the base of your Dorset knob.

2. Make an even number of blanket stitches around the base.

3. Working from the base up, sew detached blanket stitches (i.e. not into the mould) into the foundation round of blanket stitches.

4. When you reach the top, pass the needle back through the centre of the knob, bringing it out at the base. Either tie off the ends or use them to attach it to a fabric.

Button madness

As you can see from the examples above and below, the technique doesn't have to be limited to buttons. Instead of curtain rings, why not make supersized wheels using embroidery hoops? Instead of thread, use strips of plastic bags joined with decorative tape to make a dreamcatcher-style mobile.

Or perhaps make a mobile to hang above a baby's crib? For this, use soft strips of fabric in muted colours and sew them together with a couple of stitches, then roll into small balls of yarn. Make sure you work with small balls of yarn, though, or you won't be able to fit them between the spokes.

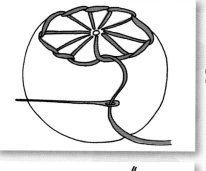

2

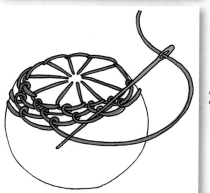

3

Pass the needle through each detached buttonhole stitch.

"Buttons and patches and the cold wind blowing,
the days pass quickly when I am sewing." – Anon

MORE THAN STITCHES

Less isn't necessarily more – there are times when you want your work to be a rich tapestry of fabric and thread. Fortunately, all it takes to achieve that sumptuous wow factor is a little know-how about fabric manipulation and embellishment.

SHIBORI

Meaning to wring, squeeze or press, *shibori* is a Japanese dyeing technique. Typically indigo is used, although not always. A limitless array of surface designs can be achieved depending on the skill of the dyer and how they manipulate the cloth. The longer the cloth is left in the dye bath, the more intense the contrast will be between the colour and the areas that have resisted the dye.

Indigo dyeing does, however, require more space and facilities than most of us have access to. If space is limited, or blue isn't your colour, an ordinary sachet of clothes dye will do, such as the tulip red I've used on these samples. Start by looking at examples of *shibori* (an internet search will provide thousands of images) and try to work out how the patterns have been achieved. As you learn to recognise various styles of *shibori*, you'll start to understand how you can replicate them in your work. To begin with, your own results might rely more on serendipity than skill, but in time you'll be able to control and predict your results.

Choosing and preparing fabric

It is best to use natural fibres such as cottons, silks or wools. Even if the fabric you are using is brand new, you will need to scour it before it can be dyed. Scouring is a form of deep cleaning that removes impurities like starch, wax or oil from the fabric. If you don't scour your fabric, the dye is unlikely to penetrate evenly and you may end up with a patchy result.

Cloth has been wrapped around hazelnuts and secured with elastic bands to produce *kanoko shibori*.

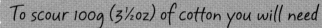

To scour 100g (3½oz) of cotton you will need

A washing machine

A 10 litre (350 fl oz) stainless steel saucepan with a lid

35g (1¼oz) of soda ash

1. Wash your fabric in a washing machine, on a long setting with very hot water. Ensure that any detergents you add do not contain bleach or fabric conditioners.

2. Half-fill the pan with water and bring to the boil. Slowly add the soda ash and when the bubbles have subsided, carefully place the still wet fabric in the pan.

3. Turn the heat to moderate and half cover the pan with its lid. Every fifteen minutes or so, give the contents a stir. After two hours, remove the fabric from the water – you'll be in for quite a surprise at just how dirty the water can be. If the water is really filthy you may need to repeat the process; otherwise dry and press your fabric as usual.

From left to right: a strip of fabric was folded concertina-style, then clamped with bulldog clips; a strip was twisted, then twisted again, until it curled around on itself – this too was held in place with clips; a ruffle was partially draped over the dye pot, allowing the fabric to soak up the dye where it came into contact.

Once you've scoured your fabric you can begin experimenting with *shibori* techniques. Here are a few suggestions to help you on your way:

A piece of fabric was folded into a fan, concertinaed along the length of the fan and secured with bulldog clips for a modern take on *itajime shibori*.

The fabric was pleated and its edges sewn tightly together to create this *nui* style. Once dry, I unpicked the stitching to reveal fine rows of bead-like patterns.

SIX *SHIBORI* TECHNIQUES

KANOKO Similar to tie-dye, fabric is bound with thread or elastic bands. This technique usually produces circular patterns.

MIURA A hook and needle are used to pluck sections of cloth, then thread is looped around each section twice. The thread isn't knotted but held in place by tension alone.

KUMO Fabric is wrapped around found objects and held in place with thread. Objects including beads, keys, nuts, bolts and screws all work well. This technique produces quite specific shapes.

NUI Cloth is stitched and the threads gathered tightly (with the aid of wooden dowels) to produce accurate patterns.

ARASHI Cloth is wrapped or twisted on its diagonal around wooden or copper poles (plastic piping available from plumber's merchants is also suitable). This technique is recognisable by its diagonal pattern.

ITAJIME A shape-resistant technique where fabric is folded and sandwiched between two pieces of wood. How fabric is folded will determine the effect, so it is worth experimenting with various ways of folding. Traditionally, wooden sticks or shapes would have been used but all manner of clamps and even CDs are now employed for this technique.

PLEATS, FOLDS AND PINCHES

The beauty of pleating or folding fabric is that it adds volume to something that is flat. Stitches may add colour and texture to cloth, but if you want your work to be more than two-dimensional, having at least a couple of pleating and folding techniques in your repertoire is essential.

A tailor or dressmaker understands the importance of pleats and darts – after all, they spend their working lives manipulating flat pieces of cloth to cover and flatter the curves of the human body. The best deliberately use pleats or folds to create air between layers of cloth and form shapes that either skim the body (think of Mariano Fortuny) or define and exaggerate it (think of Alexander McQueen).

Pleating or folding works well on a range of textiles – not just fashion items – and as well as its visual appeal it has other benefits too. Unlike gathering, which can be haphazard, pleating is easy to control and allows you to add structure exactly where it is wanted. It also adds elasticity to fabric, especially on very finely pleated satins or silks. The thing with pleats and folds is that once you start playing around with them, a whole world of possibilities opens up. Yet, in the same way that we probably use only one or two of dozens of stitch settings available on a sewing machine, we tend to use only a couple of styles of pleats in our textile projects. An entire library could be filled with all there is to say about pleats, folds, puckers and pinching, while the samples shown here barely touch the hem of the subject. I hope, at least, they will get you started on your pleating and folding odyssey.

Knife pleats

The most basic pleat, and the one I tend to use most, is the knife pleat (see diagram 1, below). Like all pleats, it gobbles up fabric, so you'll need to allow at least three times the amount of fabric than the intended size of your finished sample. Space the fold lines equidistantly, then marry up line 3 with line 1, line 6 with line 4, then line 9 with line 7, and so on. Fold lines 2, 5 and 7 should be at the back of the work, and falling to the right; all other folds should be falling to the left (see side view artwork, below).

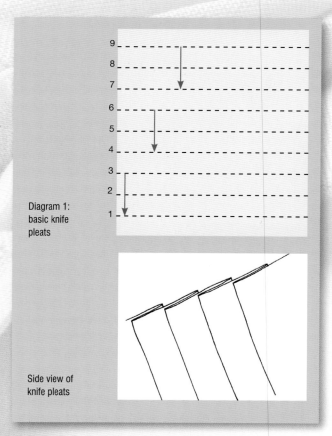

Diagram 1: basic knife pleats

Side view of knife pleats

Undulating rows

Sew each end of the knife pleat sample to secure the pleats, then divide your work into columns. On alternate columns sew in the direction of the pleats but on other columns push the pleats in the opposite direction and sew in place.

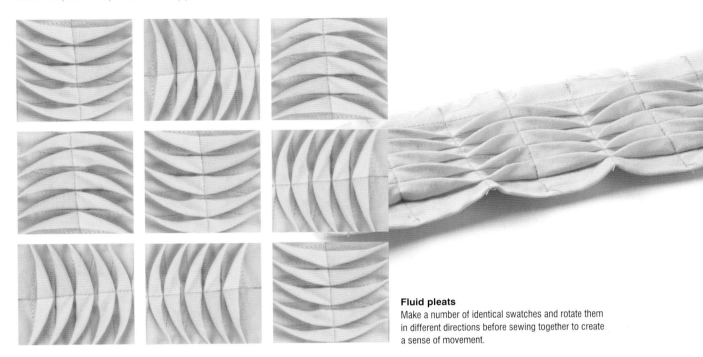

Fluid pleats
Make a number of identical swatches and rotate them in different directions before sewing together to create a sense of movement.

Or you could simply sew the pleats in one direction on one side of the swatch but in the opposite direction on the other side.

Adapting knife pleats

When you've mastered the basic knife pleat, see what else you can do with the technique. The pages of this book (far right) were made with randomly spaced pleats (see diagram 2). I took a book that was falling to pieces and made a collage from some of the pages by ironing fusible interfacing onto the reverse sides. I randomly pleated the collage, sewed the pleats in place, then added more pleats, with some crossing over the original pleats. Finally, I added further stitch embellishment.

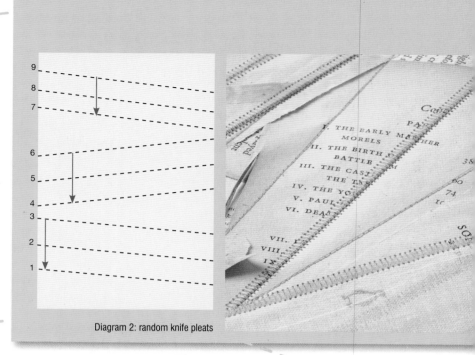

Diagram 2: random knife pleats

Elsewhere...

Look at Issey Miyake's almost sculptural use of pleats. High-quality polyester garments are cut and sewn up at three times their finished size, then pleated using a heat process to make pleats permanent, and thus easy to care for and wear

Pinches

The easiest technique of all is simply pinching fabric and sewing the pinches in place. You can still add volume and shape to fabric but in a less structured way than you would by pleating or folding. Best of all, if you run out of fabric, stop pinching!

Folds

Pleating isn't difficult to get the hang of, but simpler still is straightforward folding. The crispness of this organdie cotton was perfect for folding into a fan as it holds its shape so well. Before I folded the organdie, I divided the fabric into rows using a water-soluble pen. When the fabric was folded, I sewed the folds together on alternate rows (see diagram 3) to create a honeycomb effect.

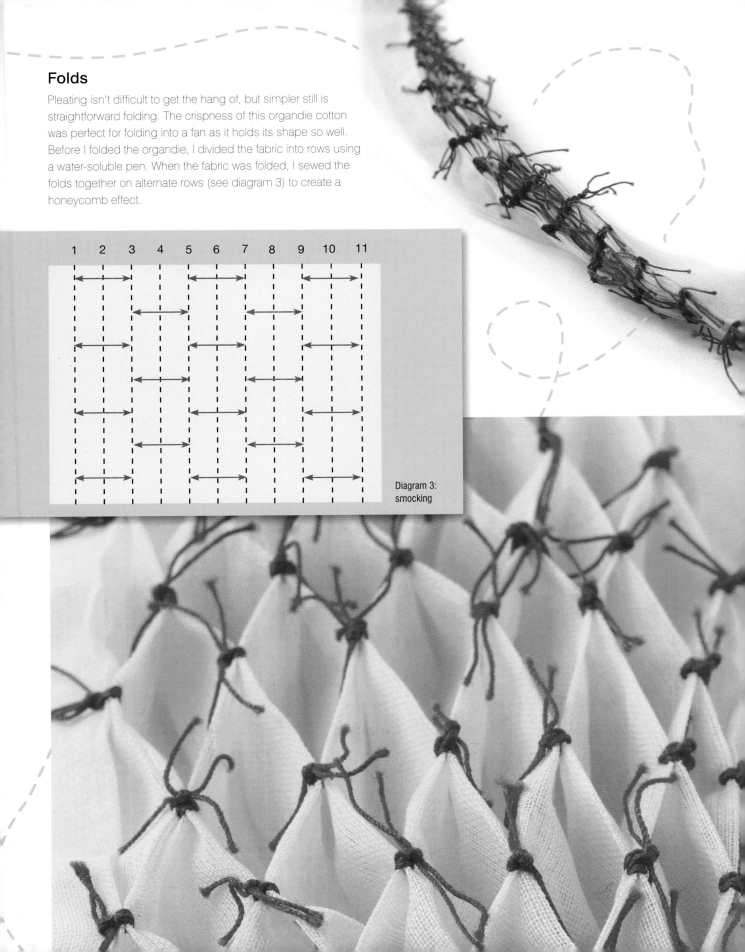

Diagram 3: smocking

TEXTURE AND ILLUSION

We all have our own favourite things about sewing and textiles. For some it's the opportunity to play with colour and pattern, for others it's the satisfaction of mastering intricate stitching – for me it's all about texture! Unlike pleats and folds, which really do create form and dimension, texture can give the illusion of a textile having more depth than it has in reality.

APPLIQUÉ

Appliqué doesn't have to mean cute or folksy. Borrowed from the French, appliqué translates as *applied*, and, in sewing terms, can be taken to mean pretty much anything that is applied to a base fabric to decorate it or create a pattern.

Appliqué circles

For years I huffed and puffed with frustration whenever I tried to turn a hem on a circle so that it wouldn't fray but would still retain its perfectly round shape. If only I'd learnt this trick sooner!

1. Draw two same-size circles – one on a piece of fusible interfacing, the other on the fabric you want to use for the appliqué. Make sure you have added a 5mm (¼in) seam allowance to each circle. Make a cross slit in the centre of the interfacing circle.
2. Place the wrong side of the fabric and the fusible side of the interfacing together and sew around the inner circle. Snip into the seam allowance every few inches all the way around, to reduce the seam's bulk.
3. Push the fabric through the slit of the interfacing and use a blunt-tipped utensil to gently ease the seam into a smooth curve. Iron your appliqué circle onto the backing fabric. For extra depth, stuff the circle with a little wadding/batting before fusing it to the background.

Appliqué diamonds

Squares of felt were folded in half along their diagonal and partially hand sewn to a background. Placing the folded squares back to back and allowing the unsewn halves to stand proud made for a scaly effect that I could see working well on a dinosaur costume for a child's fancy dress party.

Appliqué scales

Talking of scales… here, dozens of silk organdie circles were sewn to a suedette backing. As they were sewn only along their top edge, the 'scales' move when brushed. This technique would work equally well as an all-over surface texture on a sheer dress or blouse, and would help preserve some modesty, too! To create this effect, start with the bottom row and work up. On each successive row, move the position of the circles either to the right or left to replicate the staggered, scale-like effect.

Cut and twisted

Cutting and twisting works best on fabrics that have a little stiffness about them: crisp organdies, felt and leather work well, and man-made fabrics like suedette, rubber or plastic are ideal, especially if you're after an edgier look. The best results are often the simplest, for example when a single colour is used, or a slit in one layer of fabric reveals a highly contrasting colour in a layer below. That said, working with tones of a similar colour can also produce interesting effects.

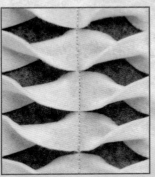

This sample is inspired by an image of a cross-section of crystal. Several layers of slightly iridescent cotton were sewn together after a series of progressively smaller arches were cut into them.

Twisted strips of felt are attached at either end to a background of matching fabric.

Slits were made in the top layer of felt then twisted and sewn in place to reveal a contrasting colour of felt below.

Semi-circles were cut into a layer of felt then lightly pressed to one side to reveal a darker suedette backing fabric.

Frayed and raw

You don't have to be a punk or a fashionista to embrace deliberately cut and frayed fabric. Distressed fabric has a wonderfully tactile quality that is hard to resist. Moreover, as age only adds to its appeal there's no need to worry about the odd thread or two shedding – natural wear and tear will make the fabric look more authentic.

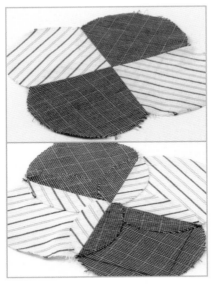

In this sample, strips of silk, tufts of fleece and organza ribbon were sewn into longer strips. I left a long tail at the end of each strip then pulled it to form a ruffle. The ruffles were then sewn onto a silk taffeta backing.

Here, knife pleats were sewn along the horizontal where two fold lines met to stop the pleats from falling apart when cut into. Cuts, just a few millimetres apart, were made along the unsewn edge of the pleating taking care not to cut into the stitching below. The sample was then washed and brushed, to encourage fraying and create more texture.

Large circles surrounding squares were sewn together along the sides of each square. When looked at from one side, you see a conventional patchwork of squares, but when looked at from the other side, a cathedral window raw edge patchwork is revealed.

WORN AND LOVED

Virtually indestructible, rag books are made from cloth designed to withstand all manner of ill-treatment at the hands (and mouths) of babies and toddlers. Nursery rhymes, counting and spelling games and simple stories are popular, and are usually illustrated with bold and colourful images, intended to stimulate and hold a child's attention.

Time and wear and tear only add to the appeal of rag books, and rare or vintage examples have become highly collectible textile items. I like to make my own rag books and use them not to help me learn my alphabet or mental arithmetic, but to practise stitches or doodle with thread when I don't fancy immersing myself in a 'big project' but still want to do a little light sewing.

The pages of the rag book shown on these pages are cut from a Hungarian linen grain sack that is covered with off-cuts and remnants from much-loved clothes and fabrics. Some of the fabrics come from my husband's old shirts, and although they really were past their best, it seemed a shame to bin them when they evoked so many memories.

As well as fabrics, I like to keep labels, which maintains a typographic link with the original rag books but also reminds me of special occasions – such as an item of clothing I wore to my wedding. The inclusion of selvedges also brings a typographic element to the book and carries vital information about the fabric such as its name, origin, composition and breakdown of colours – especially useful if it needs to be matched to other fabrics or paints in a colour scheme. To assemble the pages, I used the same method as I did for the saddle-stitched notebook on pages 46–47.

Sometimes I bind the edges of the pages (here a few have been bound with sailors' whipping twine) but more often I just let them fray. I don't mind that over time they might disintegrate and fall to pieces. If they do, I can always add in another swatch or repair a hole with some more stitching; rag books like these are never truly finished – they just get better with age. How flush all the edges are is also not an issue – the very nature of coarse fabrics like these grain sacks means they'll never fold as neatly as crisp sheets of paper. For me, it is the *wabi sabi* (imperfect and incomplete) nature of these textiles that is often at the heart of their appeal – seeing their signs of age and knowing that they have been used transforms them into a diary of things we have worn and loved or that have been worn by the people we love.

Ragpaper

Indian khadi paper is made from rags – often recycled t-shirts – and it is the long fibres of the rags that gives the paper its unique strength and durability. Why not try making a rag book out of this extraordinary fabric?

Try.....

Vintage rag books can be purchased relatively inexpensively on popular auction sites and make ideal stitch sketchbooks if you don't want to make your own rag book from scratch.

MOLA REVERSE APPLIQUÉ

For the Kuna Indians, the *mola* is much more than a decorative shirt – it is a symbol of cultural identity and a reminder of their struggle to gain political freedom.

The Kuna Indians live on a chain of islands (one for each day of the year!) called the San Blas Archipelago, which is situated on the Atlantic coast of Panama. In 1925, the Kuna people revolted against the Panamanian government, which was discouraging the use of their native language in favour of Spanish, and generally suppressing their culture in an attempt to Westernise them. Eventually, after much bloodshed, the government relented and the Kuna won the right to govern themselves, and their territories, autonomously.

Theirs is a matriarchal society and one that believes in the absolute importance of the continuance of tribal customs. Women still wear traditional dress, which consists of a blouse with two panels of *mola* reverse appliqué incorporated into its design, patterned headscarves and sarongs, gold nose rings and brightly coloured bands of beads on their ankles and arms. The Kuna men, on the other hand, have adopted Western fashion and look really quite drab in comparison to their colourfully dressed and bejewelled womenfolk.

The *mola* (meaning shirt or clothing) is thought to have its origins in body painting. It was only after colonisation by the Spanish, and no doubt due to contact with Western missionaries, that the same designs made their way from skin to cloth. Initially the designs were quite abstract (as had been the body art) but with time other motifs worked their way into *mola* designs. Another feature commonly found in *molas* is the mirroring of motifs. This relates to the concept of *acala* and a belief that everything comes in pairs – like left and right, or man and woman – and that everything is the same, but different. The Kuna people may be fierce protectors of their culture but this doesn't mean they are insular or uninterested in the outside world! While themes from nature remain popular, so are cultural and political motifs, and it is not uncommon to see *molas* that depict historical events, such as the building of the Panama canal, or characters from cartoons and advertisements. As well as their own exotic appeal to tourists, the Kuna recognise the value of their handicrafts and now cater specifically to Western tastes. Mobile phone covers and mug cosies featuring *mola* work are just two of the items the Kuna make for the tourist market.

The process

Mola reverse appliqué is, as the name implies, the opposite to conventional appliqué where layers are added to a base to form a design. In *mola* reverse appliqué, several layers of brightly coloured cloth are sewn together and a design drawn onto the top layer (although some women are so adept at *mola* work they don't even need to draw the design – they just work freehand). Sharp scissors are then used to carefully cut shapes out of the layers. The largest shapes are typically cut from the top layer, then increasingly smaller shapes cut as the sewer works her way through the layers. Scraps of fabric can be slipped between layers to introduce more colour to the work. The edges of the layers are then turned under and sewn in place with matching threads.

The best *mola* work will have stitches that are almost invisible, although they can feature additional embroidery too. The number of layers, and playful skilfullness with the cutting sequence (i.e. sometimes cutting through several layers at once to make a colour seem nearer the surface than it actually is) are a hallmark of quality, and naturally affect the price.

What's in a name?
The Kuna people successfully lobbied the
Panamanian government to be officially recognised
as Guna, since their own language doesn't
contain a 'K' sound.

MOLA: CHICKEN OR EGG?

Among my collection of tiles is this one of a chicken (right). Its geometric design seemed to lend itself perfectly to a piece of *mola* reverse appliqué, but I didn't want to follow the tile too slavishly and simply copy an existing pattern. So I made a few modifications for my *mola* motif. But the question is: which will come first, the chicken or the egg?

You will need

You can of course come up with your own design – something that is personal to you. However, If you prefer to make a version of my *mola* chicken, you will need the following:

Template, see page 153

Several layers of cotton
   (all the same size)

Sharp scissors

Tweezers (optional)

Needle

Threads in assorted colours

Water-soluble pen

Pins

1. Press your fabrics to remove any creases. Transfer the design to the fabrics, in exactly the same place each time (see page 119 for advice on using the fabric's registration marks to help you achieve this). Tack/baste the layers together around their outer edge, ensuring you haven't introduced any folds or puckers along the way.

2. On the top layer, about 1cm (½in) all the way around the design, add a border of tacking/basting stitch to prevent the design sliding or flapping about and losing its shape once you cut into the fabrics. Mark the design line with a water-soluble pen; you will cut about 5mm (¼in) inside this line. With a sharp pair of scissors, cut into the first layer of fabric. So I don't accidentally cut into the layer beneath, I find it helps to pull the layers apart with a set of tweezers. The fabric that you reveal at this stage is generally the largest area of the design: in the case of the chicken, its body; in the case of the demonstration, the dark blue rectangle. Turn the edges under then pin and sew in place. For curved shapes, snip into this seam allowance to allow the fabric to follow the curve of the design; for square shapes, snip into each corner. Cut into the second layer to reveal the fabric beneath: in the case of the chicken it was the egg; in the case of the demo, it's the red square.

3. As before, turn under the edges and sew in place. Continue to work in this way until your work is complete, but don't cut into the bottom layer. You can always create the illusion of having another layer under the bottom layer, by including two pieces of the same coloured fabric in your 'sandwich'. Simply place one higher up in the sandwich that you can cut into and then see other colours behind it.

4. In traditional *mola*, all layers are supposed to be perfectly smooth and corners neat and sharp. Puckered fabric is a no-no, and stitching is meant to be virtually invisible. However, I couldn't resist adding some colourful *kantha*-style stitching to my appliqué, so puckering is an inevitability I'm happy to accept.

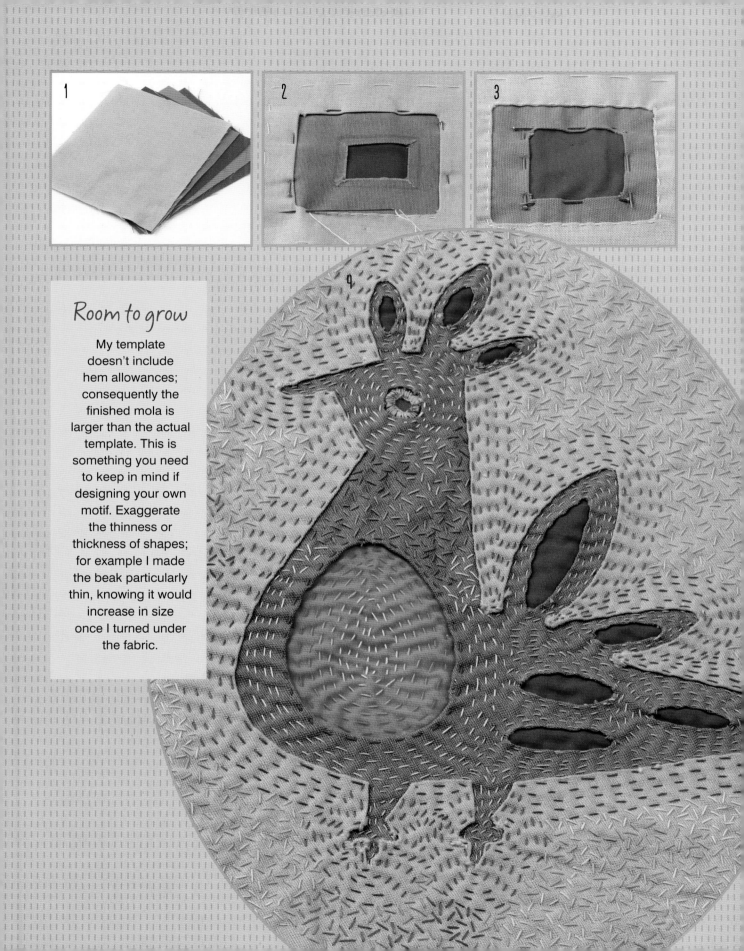

Room to grow

My template doesn't include hem allowances; consequently the finished mola is larger than the actual template. This is something you need to keep in mind if designing your own motif. Exaggerate the thinness or thickness of shapes; for example I made the beak particularly thin, knowing it would increase in size once I turned under the fabric.

CHEAT'S *MOLA*

If the idea of reverse appliqué appeals to you, but turning under all the fiddly edges doesn't, then cheat's *mola* is for you. For this you will need everything from the previous list but substitute the cotton with several squares of felt (again, all the same size). For the yellow base layer, I used a kitchen cloth.

Work in exactly the same way you would for conventional reverse appliqué, but in this instance you might want to adapt the template and thicken certain areas, as you won't be turning the fabric under, and thus increasing the size of the shape.

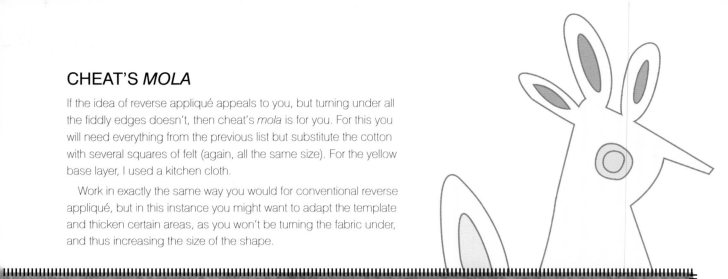

Elsewhere...
Want to create your own design but stuck for inspiration? Take a look at the graphic posters of Saul Bass, or Blue Note album covers of the 1950s and 1960s

Hitting the register

The selvedges of fabric always contain the printer's registration marks. A registration mark is usually a circle with a cross through it, and the printer uses them to make sure all the overlapping colours are in the right place. If they get it wrong, the colours look out of sync and the effect is slightly dizzying; when the printer hits the register correctly, each overlapping colour is directly on top of the other.

Try using registration marks to ensure that all your fabric layers overlap correctly. Don't get bogged down with trying to correctly align the entire image from one layer to the next. Instead, add a registration mark to the top left-hand corner and bottom right-hand corner of your template, and copy this along with the rest of the motif onto your layers of fabric. If the registration marks marry up, then so will the rest of your design.

Now which comes first, the chicken or the egg?

In conventional appliqué you add shapes to a base fabric. For this variation you can use the same template as before but this time you will cut out each of the components separately and cover each one with a scrap of fabric that is 5mm (¼in) bigger all the way round. This is so you can turn the excess over to the back of the template and sew it in place. I secured mine with blanket stitch and left the paper templates in place to help hold the shape. If you were making an appliqué that is to be worn and washed, you would need to remove the paper templates, or draw the shapes directly onto the fabrics and hem them. This isn't as simple as it sounds, as fabric on its own is quite floppy, and achieving a result that doesn't look awkward or clumsy requires a great deal of patience, dexterity and attention to detail. Finally, I surrounded my chicken with a few daisies and a ric-rac egg.

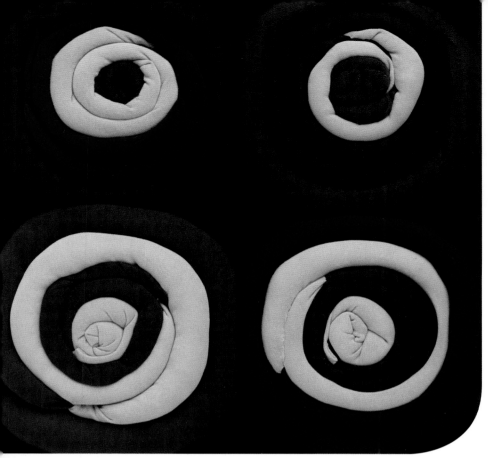

CHUNKY ROULEAUX SWIRLS

Rouleaux, as the name implies, are rolls, or tubes, of fabric often used as a trimming in millinery and couture dressmaking. *Rouleaux* don't have to be fiddly or delicate though – try supersizing them to create a fun piece of Op wall art.

Rouleaux can be padded and formed into shapes to add surface decoration to garments, left unpadded to create spaghetti straps for a lightweight dress or they can be coiled to make frogged buttons like those found on Chinese jackets. Milliners especially seem to love *rouleaux* – whether for creating unusual hat forms or for adding sculptural embellishment to classic hat styles. It is most likely, however, that you'll have come across *rouleaux* as button loops on the back of a wedding dress.

Although simple to make, *rouleaux* require a lot of fabric as they must be cut on the bias to give them their necessary flexibility. Consequently, the addition of *rouleaux* to a garment tends to denote a reasonable budget and an attention to detail usually found only in couture sewing. When you consider the impossibility of doing up the buttons on a back of a bridal gown by oneself, perhaps *rouleau* loops also allude to a time when the rich didn't dress themselves and had the luxury of being able to take as much time as they liked over their toilette.

Rouleaux can have other applications besides the worlds of *haute couture* and millinery and you can find inspiration for how you might interpret them almost anywhere. I'm a great admirer of textile artist Barbara Brown and her Op Art patterns. The almost three-dimensional effect of *Frequency* reminds me of bunched-up lengths of rope but it was *Recurrence* (and a tray of Chelsea buns!) that provided the real inspiration for my chunky *rouleaux* swirls (shown above).

Elsewhere...

To see more Op Art, look at the work of Barbara Brown, Bridget Riley, Richard Allen and Victor Vasarely

You will need

An assortment of fabrics:
  I used jersey because of its
  stretchiness

Toy stuffing

Basic sewing kit

A safety pin

1. Cut your fabric into 10cm (4in) wide strips along the bias.

2. With the wrong sides of fabric facing, fold and pin the strips in half lengthways. Sew a 5mm (¼in) seam along the long open edge, leaving a very long thread tail for turning your *rouleau* cord through the right way, and for sewing in ends. Tie the tail to a safety pin, then begin to feed the pin through the tube – the tube will start to turn in on itself. Keep easing the safety pin through the tube and when it emerges from the other end, take hold of the tail and pull until the tube is completely turned the right way out, with the seam hidden on its inside.

3. Use the long tail of thread to sew one short end of the tube together.

4. Start to fill the cavity with toy stuffing. Use a little less to begin with, as it will be harder to form the swirl if it is too overstuffed at this point.

To create the *rouleau* swirl, roll the sewn tube end in on itself a couple of times to form its core and secure with a couple of neat little stitches at the back of the work. Keep coiling and stuffing the *rouleau*, securing it with overstitch at the back of the work. When you want to add in new colours, simply overlap unstuffed ends of the *rouleau* and stitch them together, making sure that any raw edges, lumps and bumps are well tucked in and out of sight. Continue to stuff the next *rouleau*, as you did in step 4. Repeat until your swirl reaches the desired size.

Tip

If using slippery fabrics such as silk, pin a sheet of tissue paper to the top of them and sew through both layers. This will help prevent the silk from sliding about and it can be torn away quite easily after use.

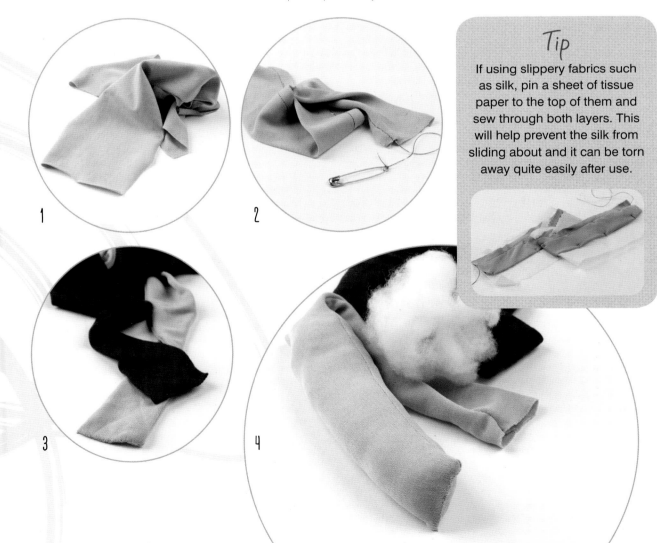

1

2

3

4

DRAWN THREAD

In drawn thread work, warp and/or weft threads are removed from even-weave fabric by cutting into it at counted intervals. The remaining threads are then bound together in groups and secured with decorative stitches to form lace-like patterns.

Elsewhere...
For a modern take on drawn thread embroidery, see the work of fashion and textile designer Susana Borobia

Often confused with pulled thread work – where instead of cutting into the fabric, holes are formed by manipulating the fabric's tension with stitches – both drawn and pulled thread work come under the umbrella of whitework embroidery. This is because they were traditionally worked in white thread on white fabric, making them a popular decorative feature for domestic linens such as handkerchiefs, bed linen, night wear and table linen.

European whitework

The Portuguese are famed for their exquisite drawn thread work but they are not alone in favouring whitework techniques. In Norway, *Hardanger* embroidery (named after the fjord and surrounding area) is popular, and consists of blocks of satin stitch often grouped around cut work. The result is a richly textured and sculptural form of embroidery that can be found on Norwegian national dress. The Italians are known for *reticella*, which is a form of drawn thread work onto which highly elaborate lace patterns are stitched. *Broderie Anglaise*, although originating in Eastern Europe, became associated with England due to its popularity there during the 19th century.

As in many other styles of embroidery, depictions of nature are popular in drawn thread work. However, it is the abstract and geometric potential that appeals to me. Embroiderers love embroidering flora and fauna but I do sometimes wonder if this isn't in part due to a quirk of sewing: we spend so much time looking down at our work that we forget to look up and see the inspiration that surrounds us, so tend to repeat well-known motifs. While the satisfaction of successfully completing an intricate design in stitch can't be denied, there are other sources of inspiration besides nature!

Why not take inspiration from the man-made world? The blue and white sample below, worked on 18-count Aida fabric, was inspired by Metro Central Heights, a development of flats in southeast London, designed by modernist architect Ernõ Goldfinger. Aida fabric is perfect for drawn thread embroidery as it's designed to make it easy for you to count and be consistent with the number of threads you pick up.

Here, I started with a four strand outer square, overcast with buttonhole stitch. Then I divided the square into columns and created the eleven vertical beams by binding them with buttonhole stitch – in fact I used buttonhole stitch throughout. Next I divided the work into rows and bound each (fourteen in total) with stitch. Then came the fun part where I started to cut into the fabric in order to remove the threads: sharp scissors and a pair of tweezers are essential here! Where I wanted the blue to show through, I cut away both the warp (vertical) and weft (horizontal) threads, but where I wanted to introduce more columns into the rows, I removed only some of the warp stitches and bound the remaining with stitch.

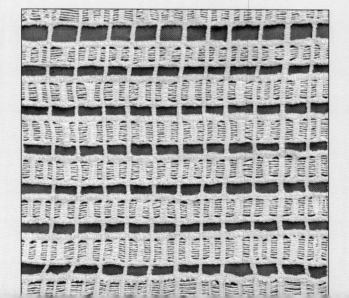

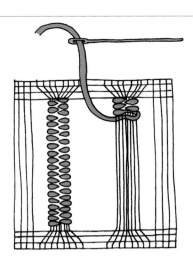

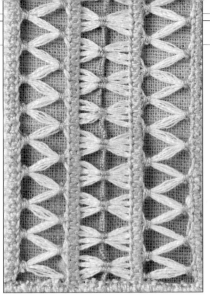

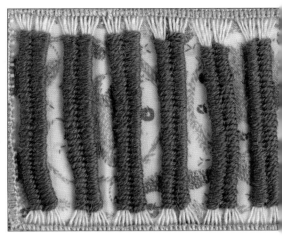

How to needle weave

Working from right to left, take your needle over the first set of four strands and under the next set of four strands. Then working from left to right, take your needle over the first set of strands and under the next set. Continue to work back and forth in this way until you've filled the desired area.

I used a thicker coloured thread to create the frame and row dividers in this sample, then removed all of the weft threads but only some of the warp threads to create even gaps between the remaining warp threads. On the middle row I grouped the threads into bunches of three to form little haystacks. The zigzag pattern on the other two rows is made by sewing two groups of strands together along one side, then alternate groups of two on the other side.

The final swatch is worked on a piece of coarse linen (almost sacking weight) backed with a colourful piece of fabric. I stitched a binding box as before but removed all of the weft threads this time. Due to the much coarser texture of this linen, I used scraps of fairly thick knitting yarn to needle weave two groups of four strands together at a time.

Look around…

As well as solitary buildings, why not take inspiration from cityscapes, construction sites, metal walkways and even stacks of boxes and palettes in warehouses? All contain grid-like imagery that is ideal for reinterpretation in drawn thread work – especially if you are new to the technique.

MARRIAGE QUILTS

A keen needlewoman (or man for that matter) might use a needle and thread to express love for a home, family or friends, but the quilts that are made to celebrate a wedding will reveal the most about their hopes, desires and values.

Although there is doubt over the actual number, some quilt historians believe that it was common practice during the 19th century for a young girl to make thirteen quilts as part of her trousseau. Twelve of the quilts would be for everyday use but the thirteenth would be for special occasions, such as her marriage. The thirteenth quilt had to be made by the bride alone and finished on the eve of her wedding. Once the quilt was complete, the original pattern would be destroyed as it now belonged only to the bride and groom. The style of the quilt was generally either an appliqué or a whole cloth quilt and would be decorated with symbols of love and fertility, such as flowers, birds and intertwined vines. Presumably, the number of quilts was both a testament to the bride-to-be's productivity and provided an opportunity as she sewed to contemplate her future life as a wife and homemaker. It's hard to verify exactly how many quilts a bride was expected to make as due to the nature of domestic textiles, they inevitably fall to pieces the more they are used, so surviving examples are rare.

A surviving exception is the quilt made to commemorate the marriage of Mary Parker of Crediton in 1770, although it is not known if she made the quilt herself. For her bridal quilt, silk ribbons and plain weave fabrics are combined into a patchwork of multicoloured quarter-square triangles, pinwheels and pink and yellow sashing. It is wadded with wool, then quilted with a sun-like motif, flowers and trailing leaves. Another surviving example of a bride's quilt is the one made to celebrate the marriage of John Haldeman and Anna Reigart in 1846. It is composed of twenty-five sunburst blocks, sashings and a border. Each of the blocks was

made and signed by a member of the respective families and some close friends. This was common practice and a means of recognising the union of not just two people, but also their families. Also known as signature quilting, this was a particularly popular form of quilting in America, but cottons, rather than silks, would be used for the patchwork.

In times gone by, the wealthy and important would have others make their bridal quilts for them. It's hard to imagine Marie Antoinette having the patience or discipline to make her own wedding quilt but it's no surprise that her expectations for owning only the best meant that it took eight needlewomen over a hundred hours to produce her *broderie de Marsailles* wedding quilt. *Broderie de Marsailles* is an exquisite style of quilting that uses cords and stuffing to create highly elaborate relief designs (see the example shown right). Motifs such as ripe fruits, over-spilling cornucopias, urns of magnificent flowers – basically images of abundance – are often depicted and are perfect for suggesting a fertile marriage bed.

Perhaps the most famous example of a *trapunto* wedding quilt is the Tristan quilt, part of which is owned by the Victoria and Albert (V&A) Museum in London. Although the remaining piece doesn't depict the love triangle between Tristan, Isolde and King Mark, it is thought that the whole quilt would have included that part of the legend too. Another theory is that this quilt would have been one of a pair, with a related piece hanging in the Bargello museum, Florence. Citing the legend of Tristan and Isolde would have flattered the couple to be married. It not only suggests that their union is akin to that of two of literature's greatest lovers,

"Chains do not hold a marriage together. It is threads, hundreds of tiny threads which sew people together through the years." – Simone Signoret

but with its connotations of courtly love, heroic deeds and knightly behaviour, it implies that the bride and groom are equal to great heroes and heroines of legend. Further, by bringing all this together in a quilt, the message is clear: a great dynasty will be the result of this union.

These days it would seem absurd to expect a woman to make a large number of quilts as part of a trousseau, but if she were to make a patchwork quilt to celebrate her wedding, a good choice would be something based on the traditional wedding rings design. It's not for the faint-hearted though, as it involves painstaking paper piecing and lots of curves. The results are well worth the effort as the finished pattern of interlocking rings can be quite stunning and would grace any bed.

This traditional French sample of *Broderie de Marsailles* dates to about 1890.

TRAPUNTO GRAFFITI

Whether you consider it street art or crime, there's no denying that graffiti packs a punch. In recent years, graffiti has become increasingly sophisticated, with works by artists such as the elusive Banksy fetching hundreds of thousands of dollars.

Elsewhere...

For graffiti inspiration look at the work of (believed to be) British-born Banksy, and American artist Jean-Michel Basquiat

Graffiti has come a long way since the days of 'Kilroy woz ere'– a phrase usually accompanied by a doodle of a bald man peeking over a wall, which became popular during WWII. The hip hop culture of the 1980s saw increasingly creative graffiti appear on everything from walls to buses to the subways of New York, as artists competed with each other, in much the same way as they did with their dance moves, to see who could produce the most spectacular art. Today, street art has, for some, become a business, and companies will pay good money to have paint sprayed onto the sides of their buildings by well-known graffiti artists. Nevertheless, most street art has remained true to its roots and still manages to amuse, shock or provoke – often all at the same time.

Italian inspiration

I took a photograph of some graffiti I saw at a train station in Italy (below left), as I thought it might be interesting to sew something along the same lines. I particularly wanted to reproduce the 'bubble' lettering, where heavily outlined, curvy letters overlap and crash into each other. To give them a little more oomph, I decided to stuff parts of the design from the reverse of the fabric – a technique known as *trapunto*. This resulted in my 'pop' sample, see below.

Trapunto is a technique in which two layers of fabric are sewn together, then the back piece is slit and stuffed so that areas of the design become raised. The slits are then sewn up to prevent the wadding/batting from falling out; for this reason, it's an idea to use fabrics that don't fray too easily, such as felt, for the backing. If you want to try your hand at *trapunto*, I suggest you start with something simple, like the heart project, shown right, before moving on to a more complex design, such as a piece of graffiti.

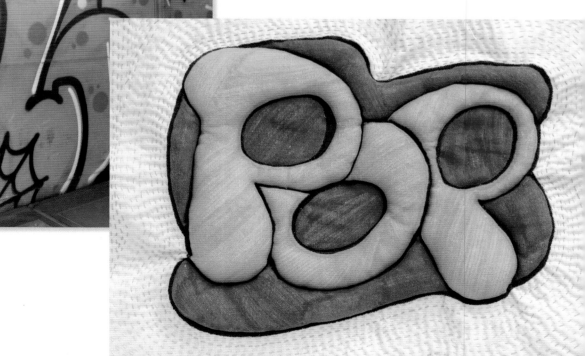

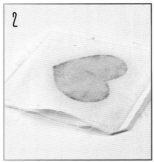

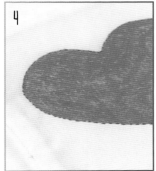

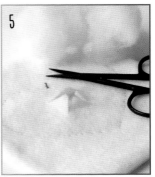

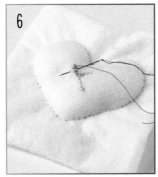

1. With a water-soluble pen, draw a heart onto the cotton layer of fabric.

2. Colour in the heart with fabric marker pen. Place the cotton and felt right sides together and sew a 5mm (¼in) seam around the edges leaving a small gap on one side so you can turn the pouch the right way through. Trim off the excess fabric at the corners so they will look crisper, and less bulky, when turned the right way round.

3. Turn the fabric the right way out and use a knitting needle or blunt pencil to poke out the corners.

4. Sew the gap shut with whip stitch. Sew around the heart with tiny running stitches.

5. Working from the back of the work, tease the layers apart – you might find a pair of tweezers useful for this. When you are sure they are separate, make a crossed slit in the heart. If you also want to stuff the border, make a few slits in that too.

6. Now stuff the cavity. Use a blunt pencil or knitting needle to help you gently poke stuffing into the corners. Be careful not to poke too hard or you might tear the fabric or rip through the stitching! When you can't squeeze in any more stuffing, and the the mound is firm when you press it, sew up the slits at the back of the work. Finally, decorate the background with colourful stitching.

GATHERED CIRCLES OF JOY

There is something almost magical about the Suffolk puff, which can transform a wedding or evening dress into a gown fit for a fairytale princess. En masse, they add texture when appliquéd onto a background fabric, but you could go Suffolk puff crazy and dispense with the background altogether and construct a fabric made entirely from these little gathered circles.

I make mine from fabrics such as silks, satins and organzas, because although simple to make, Suffolk puffs require time, and in a world where time is a luxury, a time-consuming job deserves luxury fabrics. However, they also look charming when made from inexpensive, brightly coloured solids and printed cottons. Especially when used to decorate little girls' dresses, where the addition of Suffolk puffs seems like a match made in clothes heaven. Add a cute button to its centre, and the Suffolk puff becomes even more playful and is sure to bring a smile to a child's face each time she wears the dress.

Not just for clothes

Suffolk puffs have long been used in home furnishings – 19th-century Suffolk puff quilts are a prime example of this. Humble in origin, Suffolk puff quilts, like other domestic textiles, may well have been decorative but were essentially utilitarian items driven by a need to make the most of the meagre materials available. Made from scraps of clothing and old fabrics, the puffs would be stitched together and, for added warmth, sometimes stuffed with fleece from local sheep.

Perhaps you played with a Suffolk puff clown as a child – a fabric doll whose limbs are stacks of gathered circles? Or maybe you've seen Suffolk puffs incorporated into jewellery items such as brooches, corsages or necklaces? Wherever you've seen them, and whether they were stacked, stuffed, elegantly sheer or colourfully cute, Suffolk puffs are a great feature to have in any stitcher's box of sewing tricks.

HOW TO MAKE A SUFFOLK PUFF

You will need
Fabric and a basic sewing kit

1. Decide on the eventual size you want your puff to be, then cut a circle twice that size, plus about 5mm (¼in) extra all round for hemming.

2. Using running stitch, hand sew a small, single fold hem around the edge of the circle. Do not tie off the thread.

3. Instead, gently pull the thread until the circle gathers in on itself. When you have gathered the circle as much as you can, tie off and cut the thread. Finger press the puff into shape.

Elsewhere...
- The Chanel 2010 couture show, which featured a yoyo quilt cape
- Suffolk clown dolls
- Suffolk puff quilts

"When life throws you scraps, make a quilt." – Anon

If a plain *pojagi* panel is, well, just a little too plain for your taste, you could always embellish it with a few Suffolk puffs (see pages 36–37).

NOT TO BE SNIFFED AT

There's more to a handkerchief than meets the nose. Whether used to signal the start of a duel, dropped coquettishly to attract a man's attention, or brandished by a magician as part of a conjuring trick, the handkerchief contains a wealth of history and meaning...

The history of the hanky

Linen handkerchiefs were said to have been introduced to England by King Richard II (1367–1400), but nowadays few people carry one. Instead, thanks to the Kleenex™ company (who were the first to produce a disposable tissue handkerchief in 1924), style has given way to convenience – and hygiene – and these perfect little textiles have fallen out of favour.

Yet a handkerchief is far more useful than a flimsy piece of tissue and says so much about its owner. Imagine a man sporting a handkerchief and a foppish, debonair, or aristocratic character may spring to mind. But the handkerchief has just as many sartorial connotations that are to do with the labouring classes and those up to no good! Cowboys used neckerchiefs (who can picture John Wayne without one?) to protect their faces against dust kicked up by horses and cattle. While the Native Americans, who were just as partial to a handkerchief, would happily exchange other items of trade for them. And of course, a handkerchief can be used to conceal one's true identity – as any self-respecting highwayman, bandit or burglar must know if they are to avoid detection!

Shameful trade

Some instances of handkerchiefs that are synonymous with their wearers remind us of a shameful past where people were captured, sold and treated as subhuman simply because of the colour of their skin. The Madras handkerchief – a large plaid square often worn as a turban – for example, is inextricably associated with the triangle of trade and exportation of slaves. Manufactured in Southern Indian villages, Madras handkerchiefs were exported and sold in Britain, and then used to trade for slaves in the West coast of Africa. To add insult to injury, one of the few items of clothing a female slave might be given was a handkerchief to wear as a headscarf.

In 1785, in Louisiana, the tignon laws (a tignon being a series of handkerchiefs wrapped into a turban resembling the West African *gélé*) decreed that all women of colour – slaves and free women alike – were compelled to cover their heads with scarves. This was done in attempt to maintain class and ethnic distinctions between the Spanish and women of colour.

"That handkerchief did an Egyptian to my mother give... To lose't or give't away were such perdition as nothing else could match." –
Othello, Act 4, Scene 1

A symbol of love and betrayal

Handkerchiefs, and their embellishments, have long been used as symbols of love. As mentioned earlier in this book (pages 48–49), Portuguese love hankies were lovingly embroidered handkerchiefs that a young girl would send to the object of her affection. In this case, the embroidered motifs would be the symbols of love. However, sometimes it is the handkerchief itself, or where it is placed, that can silently articulate what one wants to say. This was particularly the case among gay men during the 1970s – different coloured hankies would be placed in various pockets, or on parts of the body, to let other people know their likes, dislikes and relationship status. For Shakespeare's famously jealous lover Othello, the handkerchief is such a potent symbol of fidelity that when he finds Desdemona's handkerchief in Cassio's room, he immediately reads it as material evidence of her betrayal, for which she pays with her life.

So, the next time you receive a box of handkerchiefs as a gift, don't dismiss it as something more befitting an Edwardian spinster. Remember you are carrying around a piece of social history in your pocket. Even if you choose not to dab your nose on a freshly laundered linen handkerchief, you can always tie a knot in it as a reminder for something that needs to be done.

Elsewhere...
- Portuguese love hankies
- Portrait of Lady Anne Cecil by William Larkin, 1614–18
- Portrait of a Haitian Woman by François Malépart de Beaucourt

A CHRISTENING GIFT

We've seen the role handkerchiefs play in courtship and love, but these perfect little textiles can also be used to mark other occasions in life, such as the birth of a child or a Christening.

I made this patchwork ball from a selection of vintage handkerchiefs in my collection. Some were so frail and delicate they needed backing with linen to prevent them falling to pieces, and to lessen any showthrough of hems once the English paper pieces were removed. I wanted the ball to have plenty of texture – partly for my own satisfaction, but also to give the baby more stimulus when they play with it – so I added some *trapunto* domes, an embroidered rabbit and lots of bullion knots.

If you decide to add personal touches like these to your handkerchiefs, don't risk guessing the eventual size of your pentagons. In this instance, going freestyle is not to be recommended, as you're bound to lose some of your stitching in the seams, or find that it looks really out of proportion when you cut your fabrics. Instead, use a water-soluble pen to draw the correct sized pentagon onto your handkerchief, then clamp the handkerchief in an embroidery hoop and work within the marked area.

Elsewhere...
Take a closer look at the work of embroiderer Karen Ruane, who incorporates vintage linens into her textiles (see below)

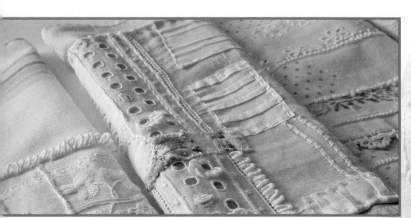

Pre-loved domestic textiles such as handkerchiefs often feature in the work of Karen Ruane. The samples shown include a man's handkerchief with a vintage lace overlay, secured with bullion knots (on the left). The blue base cloth of the middle piece is another man's handkerchief; the piece on the right is composed of a spotty handkerchief, an old handkerchief secured with hand stitching and strips of vintage cloth.

You will need

A selection of handkerchiefs

Basic sewing kit

Embroidery hoop

Water-soluble pen

Toy stuffing

Medium-weight paper

Template, see page 153 (this will give you a ball with a circumference of about 51cm (20in); scale up or down for a larger or smaller ball)

Tip: double up

If reusing drawn thread or the lace detail of a handkerchief, you'll need two pieces of fabric to wrap your template: the decorative layer along with a backing layer to keep the stuffing in place. Experiment with colour and try using a coloured backing fabric so the lace or drawn thread work really stands out.

1. Using the template on page 153, cut twelve pentagons from medium-weight paper.

2. Cut twelve pieces of fabric, making each 5mm (¼in) bigger than your template all the way round. Try to position particularly interesting elements of your handkerchief, such as a printed motif or element of embroidery, within the centre of each pentagon – this is known as fussy cutting. Wrap each paper pentagon with a pentagon of fabric and pin together. Tack/baste the fabric in place and remove the pins.

3. Arrange your pentagons into two lots of six. Decide which will be the central pentagon of each lot. Whip stitch one edge of each of the five remaining pentagons to one of the edges of the central pentagon. You will end up with two florets.

4. Whip stitch the sides of the florets together to form two cups. Remove the paper from the central pentagon of each floret, but leave all the other paper pieces where they are, for now.

5. Marry up the two cups so the peaks of one set of pentagons sit into the valleys of those on the other. Use whip stitch to sew the florets together. When you are about halfway done, begin to remove the papers from any pentagons that are bound on all sides.

6. Begin to stuff the ball and continue to whip stitch the pentagons together. When there are only a couple of edges left to sew, remove the last of the papers (you might want to pin, or tack/baste, the last two hems in place). Be sure to add plenty of stuffing to the cavity as you don't want the ball to be saggy and limp. When you are satisfied that it will be nice and plump, whip stitch the remaining two edges together and remove any remaining tacking or pins. Mould the ball into shape by hand to get it perfectly round.

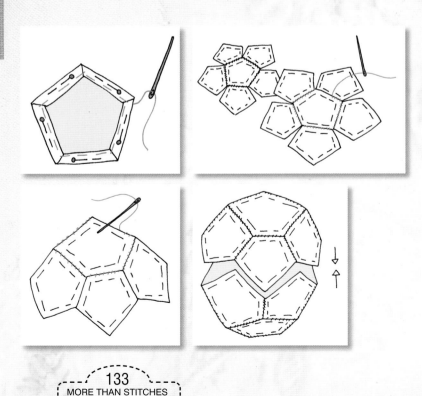

MIRROR, MIRROR

Shisha, or *sheesha*, mirror embroidery originated in Persia (modern day Iran) but made its way to India during the Mughal era. Although now produced throughout India, Gujarat is renowned for its particular excellence in *shisha* work, or *abhala bharat,* as it is also known.

Used on everything from bespoke clothing to tourist trinkets, *shisha* quality can vary according to the skill of the embroiderer. Further, since *shisha* work allows the embroiderer personal expression and rarely follows a template, you're unlikely to find two identical pieces of mirror work embroidery. Even on highstreet examples – where you might expect each garment to be an exact replica of the next – the mirror work is never the same. However, it has to be said that the quality of work in these instances is likely to be poor, with the origins and working conditions of the embroiderers unknown.

Shisha dates back to the 17th century – originally pieces of mica were used, but tin, glass, coins, and even the iridescent wings of beetles were later incorporated. Nowadays, specially produced mirrors are widely available from craft stores and online traders, and come in a range of shapes and sizes.

The mirrors are shown to their best advantage when embroidered onto a dark or neutral background that doesn't fight with the embroidery and makes the most of how they catch and reflect the light. While you'll often find the mirrors decorated with multicoloured threads, using a single, complimentary metallic thread is popular for bridal and evening wear.

STUDS AND WINKS
Instead of mirrors, tiddlywinks have been used here. Other embellishments include press studs, matt seed beads and ric rac.

HOW TO WORK *SHISHA* EMBROIDERY

You will need

A *shisha* mirror or disc

Fabric to attach the disc to

Sewing needle

Thread or your choice – I used cotton perlé

Foundation stitches

1. Form a noughts and crosses (tic tac toe) style grid over the mirror, ensuring that each time you pass a needle through the fabric it is as close as possible to the mirror. This will prevent the disc from sliding about.

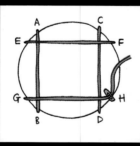

2. Rotate your work by 45° and form another grid. Your mirror should now be anchored firmly in place and you will have a lattice to work into.

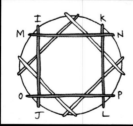

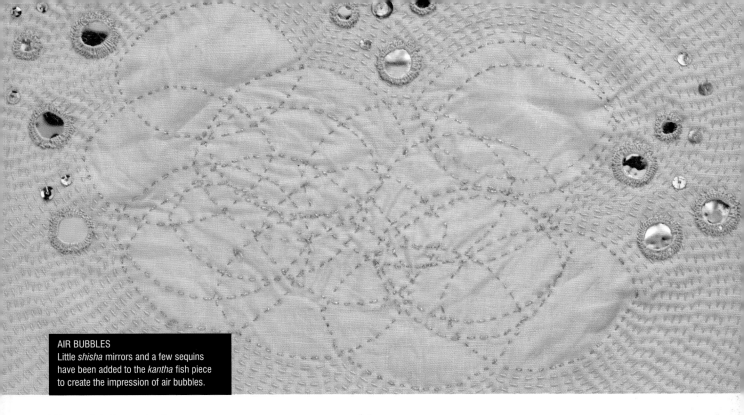

The *shisha* stitch

3. Bring up the needle through the fabric at a point very close to the mirror. Take your thread under the foundation stitches and back over them as you would if working buttonhole stitch. You should pull the stitch quite tight (not too tight though); if the foundation stitches slide off the mirror you haven't sewn them closely and tightly enough to the mirror.

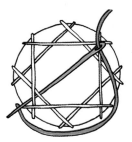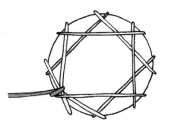

4. Take the needle down through the fabric as close to the mirror and the first stitch hole, as you can.

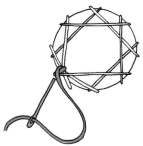

5. Don't pull the thread completely taut – instead, bring the needle back up through the fabric and loop of thread to form a tiny chain stitch. The smaller you make the chain stitch, the neater and more compact looking your *shisha* work will appear.

6. Repeat steps 3–5 until you have worked your way around the disc.

Elsewhere...

For an example of some stunning mirror work, see the 2002 Bollywood film *Devdas,* in which the actress Madhuri Dixit wears an opulent *lehnga* (bridal skirt or outfit) designed by Abu Jani Sandeep Khosla

MUDLARKING

The beach hides many treasures that are only revealed at low tide. Sometimes their value is purely decorative, at others, their archaeological significance is prized. In the past, mudlarking was considered a form of professional scavenging that could turn a pretty penny.

Until the early 20th century, mudlarking was a recognised occupation, albeit one practised mainly by the poorest of the poor. Mudlarkers would search for everything from coins and trinkets to old clothes and buttons in the hope of selling them on for a profit. Nowadays, it is mainly a pleasure pursuit – one of my favourite spots for mudlarking is along the north bank of the River Thames. Here, I get an entirely different view of the city, from a place of surprising peace and quiet.

As London was once an important trading port, finds can range from cargo fallen from passing boats to ancient antiquities such as Roman and Saxon jewellery. During the Great Fire of London (2–5 September 1666), the Thames was a route of escape. Londoners fled the city, taking whatever belongings they could carry, hurling them on to waiting boats; sometimes these would miss their mark and land in the river instead.

Tip

Should you decide to make a mudlarked textile be sure to couch your finds securely to the background. Aim to cover all sides of any fragments, especially the longest edges, otherwise they will eventually work their way loose.

Playing by the rules

There's a strong possibility you could go home with a piece of history in your pocket, but do be aware that there are strict rules governing what you can take.

- First, you can only take surface finds without needing a licence, if you do so much as turn a stone to try and unearth a tidal treasure, you will need a licence!
- Secondly, anything of archaeological significance must be handed over to the authorities.
- Thirdly, some areas do not allow mudlarking under any circumstances, so check before you disturb anything that you're not in a restricted area.
- Finally, rules vary from area to area, so don't just assume that what is fine in one place is universally applicable.

Transforming your haul

Your haul is likely to consist of fragments of pottery, or pieces of tumbled glass if you're beachcombing at the seaside. I've amassed quite a collection of delftware over the years as I love the combination of blue and white. Rather than keep all my finds in jars, I like to incorporate some of them into textiles.

The piece shown below uses a combination of silk chiffon and scrunched-up scrim to suggest the outgoing tide, and some white silk for the shoreline. Blue and white scraps of Liberty tana lawn and indigo print are used to represent fragments of pottery waiting to be mudlarked, while the burlap/hessian sacking is a nod to the Thames' trading links. For the teacup, I've used another piece of silk, onto which

I've couched pieces of delftware that I like to think might once have graced the table of Samuel Pepys!

The stitching is a combination of hand and machine stitches. I used a machine zigzag stitch around the appliquéd blue and white fabrics, and a regular running stitch for the outline of the cup. To accentuate the tide's flow and the marks it leaves on the shore, I've hand-stitched some running stitch using a cotton perlé thread. The same has been used to backstitch a few pebbles on the shore. To prevent the pieces of pottery sliding about while I couched them in place, I dabbed a spot of glue on to their reverse side, but a piece of double-sided tape would have worked just as well.

Safety first

Whether you are mudlarking along a river's shoreline or on the beach, you need to do the following:

- Check tide times!
- Start your expedition as the tide is going out, not when it is at its lowest point – this allows more time for mudlarking. Make sure you can easily exit the beach – you don't want to get cut off by an incoming tide.
- Take carrier bags for finds.
- Wear disposable gloves: rivers especially get contaminated by sewage, and can harbour diseases.
- Carry a pack of antiseptic wipes.
- Wear sensible shoes.
- Don't mudlark alone – not only is there safety in numbers, but mudlarking is more fun that way.

FIBONACCI FLOWER

Sometimes referred to as nature's numbering system, Fibonacci sequences can be found in everything from the spiral arrangement of bracts in a pine cone, to the centre of a sunflower, to the pattern made by Romanesco broccoli florets – where each individual floret mimics the pattern of the whole.

Leaves and petals also arrange themselves in Fibonacci sequences, which may explain why it's so rare to find a four-leaf clover! Rather than there being some deep mystical reason for this mathematical marvel, the explanation is probably a matter of survival: each petal is more likely to receive the light needed for the process of photosynthesis if it follows a Fibonacci sequence.

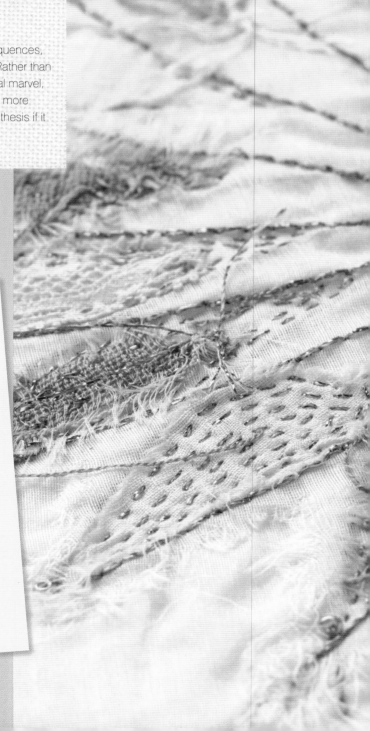

Fibonacci who?

Fibonacci, or to give him his full name, Leonardo of Pisa (1170– 1250), was an Italian mathematician who promoted the use of the Arabic numbering system in Europe. He also introduced his Fibonacci sequence to Europe (although the sequence had been known to Asian mathematicians since the 6th century AD) after studying the breeding patterns of rabbits!

The Fibonacci sequence states that any number within the sequence is the sum of two previous numbers:

$0 + 1 = 1$

$1 + 1 = 2$

$2 + 1 = 3$

$3 + 2 = 5$

$5 + 3 = 8$

$8 + 5 = 13$

And so on…

HOW TO DRAW A FIBONACCI FLOWER

You will need

Layers of fine gauzy fabric

Water-soluble pen

Protractor

Basic sewing kit

A pair of compasses, or a circular
object that you can use to draw an
arc with – a saucer or plate is ideal

1. Using a water-soluble pen, draw a
   circle on one of the layers of fabric.
   Pick a number from the Fibonacci
   sequence, for example 21, and
   divide the circle evenly into that
   many sections (in this case they
   will be 17.4° apart).

2. Working clockwise around the
   circle, draw 21 identical arcs that
   start at the centre of the circle and
   pass through the outer points of the
   circle. Gentle arcs will produce long,
   slender petals, more pronounced
   arcs will produce rounder petals.

3. Draw another set of arcs, this time
   working anti-clockwise around the
   circle so they overlap the first set to
   form petals. You now have a basic
   Fibonacci flower!

You don't have to draw both sets of
arcs on to the same layer of fabric, you
could begin your stitching after step
1 – as I did – then add another layer of
fabric before drawing the second round
of arcs. In total, I used three layers of
gauzy fabric for this piece to give it a
feeling of depth. I decorated each layer
with stitch but added beads and scraps
of lace and silk to the top layer.

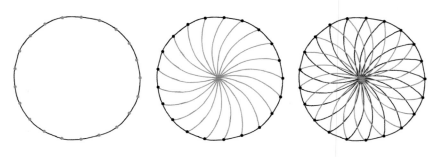

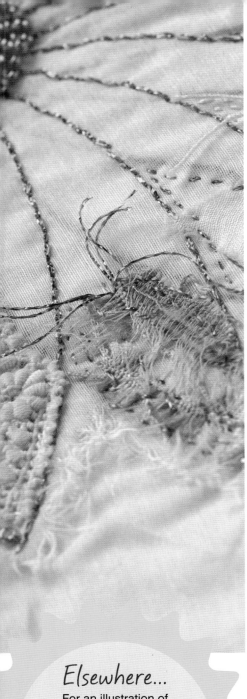

Pompom flowers

Regardless of whether you are aiming for a realistic flower or an abstract interpretation, applying the Fibonacci sequence to your design will make it more believable. If you wanted to create a more complex flower – one with more than one round of petals – here's how you would do it.

1. On a sheet of paper, draw one basic Fibonacci flower with three petals. Make this the smallest of your circles if you want the sort of pompom effect you might see in a dahlia or aster.

2. By its side, draw another, slightly larger, flower, with five petals.

3. Draw a third flower that is larger still, with eight petals. Using the Fibonacci sequence, continue drawing progressively larger circles until you have the number you're happy with.

4. Starting with the largest flower, transfer the images to fabric. When you trace the two smaller flowers, rotate them so you get an even spread of petals.

Elsewhere...
For an illustration of how prevalent the Fibonacci sequence is in nature, see the following YouTube video: Doodling in math: spirals, Fibonacci, and being a plant.

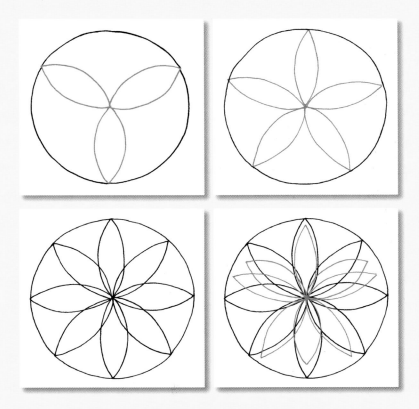

THE POOR SEWER'S EMBELLISHER

Unless you're embarking on a long series of fibre arts projects, investing in an embellishing machine may end up being the sewing equivalent of buying a fondue set. To begin with, you'll use your new toy non-stop and embellish everything in sight. The novelty will almost certainly wear off, however, and eventually, your once-loved embellisher will be consigned to the back of a cupboard to collect dust.

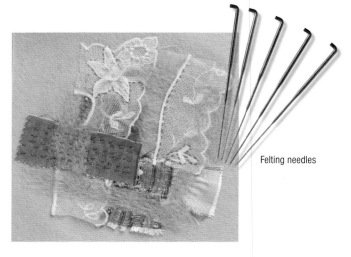

Well known for producing richly coloured and multi-layered images, felting needles and embellishing machines create just as much impact when only a single colour is used, such as on the hem of this skirt.

Felting needles

Having said that, embellisher machines are great fun to play with and, when used skilfully, produce interesting results. The main differences between an embellisher and a regular sewing machine are that you don't thread an embellisher or use a bobbin, and instead of one needle there are several – anything from five to twelve. The needles are surrounded by a guard that protects your fingers and eyes and helps to control any fibres you are adding to your base fabric. These fibres are then punched into the base fabric. The sound and action can seem quite alarming when you first use an embellisher, so start slowly, and only build up speed as your confidence grows. When it comes to fabric choices, open-weave fabrics are best, but felt is ideal as it melds beautifully with fleece and chiffons to create almost painterly effects.

If you don't have access to an embellisher machine and would like to experiment with one, but not enough to spend money on something you might only use a handful of times, there is a cheaper alternative. Felting needles, like embellisher needles, are barbed and don't have eyes, and can be used

in exactly the same way to mash fabrics together. Admittedly it's a slower, more laborious process, but the results are the very similar.

To test this out, I started by playing around with a few scraps of lace and silk, and some blue roving – the felting needles did the job just as I hoped they would (see above). For the image of the figure (see right) I used similar fabrics and felted the background, the girl's hair and the top of her skirt. I wanted some of the textured silk to show through so used the yellow roving sparingly in that area. In general, I'd recommend a light hand when adding to an image, as it's virtually impossible to remove something once it's been felted into place. Also, when you add to a base fabric, avoid adding big clumps of roving, which will just result in a lumpy and patchy mess. Aim for the thickness and transparency of a single-ply tissue and build up the layers gradually. Try adding stitch embellishment between the layers of roving, and leave some areas unembellished, as I've done on the girl's blouse.

"I don't lie, I just embellish." – Anon

Colour mixing

If you apply the fleece in thin wisps the effect is similar to that when mixing paint. For example, layering wisps of blue and yellow will produce green; add wisps of white for a weaker tint and wisps of black for a darker shade.

PAISLEY PARK

The teardrop shape of the 'botteh' (Persian for a bush, shrub or thicket) has been a standard motif in Middle Eastern and Indian textiles for centuries. It was in the 19th century, however, that the Scottish town Paisley popularised (and became forever associated with) the motif by weaving them into the shawls it produced.

While the paisley shawl may have fallen out of fashion, the paisley motif is a continual source of inspiration for designers. I like to make needle-woven appliqués based on paisley motifs, as these work well incorporated into other textiles. Perhaps the most satisfying thing about needle-woven shapes is that you are literally making something out of nothing. There is no strict pattern to work to – just a basic outline – and off you go! All you need to make a needle-woven appliqué is an enclosed shape to use as a starting point.

1. Using the template on page 156, transfer the paisley motif onto a piece of card. Use a medium-sized needle to pierce holes along the design lines.

2. Couch the design outline with yarn, using the holes you pierced in step 1; secure the yarn by sewing through the holes with contrasting thread, taking the thread over the yarn, then back through the hole.

3. As you can see here, only the anchoring threads should be visible on the back of the card; the yarn should rest on top of the card.

4. Cover the basic shape with buttonhole stitch, using the thinner thread to do so. Work the stitches closely together as you want the basic shape to be fairly rigid when it is eventually removed from the card. Be sure to cover only the yarn and don't sew through the card – if you do, it will mess up the tension, and make it much harder to remove the card later. If you need to join in new thread, make sure any ends are tied in on the underside of the yarn, not the side you can see.

5. Working into the loops on the buttonhole stitches, fill in the spaces with long stitches, as shown.

6. When you are finished, turn the card over and snip away the couching threads until you can pull the card free of your paisley shape. Remove any remaining couching threads with a pair of tweezers. Use your fingers to shape your work, then pin it to a blocking board or ironing board covered with a piece of protective cloth. Lightly spray it with starch to help set the paisley shape.

Piling it on

Try building up different layers of stitch to produce a cobweb-like effect. Also, try adding lightweight glass beads that will catch the light in case you decide to hang your shape by a window.

You will need

Medium-weight card

Template, page 156

Two different thicknesses of thread in the same colour: I used knitting yarn and cotton perlé

A contrasting colour of finer thread for securing yarn to card

A needle

Scissors

Tweezers

Spray starch and pins

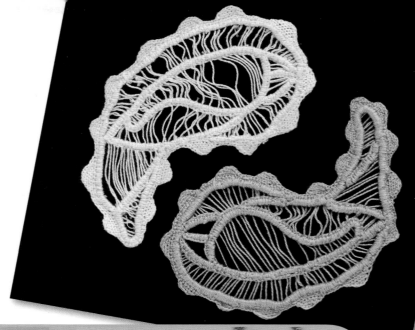

THE STITCHES

You don't need an encyclopedic knowledge of embroidery stitches and styles to produce rich and interesting work. Indeed, it is better to master a handful of well-known stitches and explore their potential. After all, if you don't fully understand the basics, you're likely to struggle with more complicated stitches.

STRAIGHT STITCHES

RUNNING STITCH

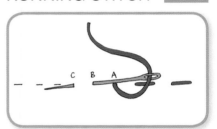

This can be used either as a filler or an edging stitch. It doesn't matter if your stitches are big or small, the important thing is that their size is consistent. There are two ways of working running stitch: for stitches that look the same on both sides of your work use a 'punch and poke' or 'stabbing' method. To do this, hold your needle perpendicular to the work so it doesn't go in at an angle when pushed through the fabric. Pull the thread through, then bring the needle back through the work, again, with it held perpendicular to the fabric to avoid creating any angles. Although this method takes practice, it allows you to produce more natural-looking and controllable curves, with evenly spaced stitches that are the same on both sides of the work, which is why many quilters like to use this technique.

The other way of working running stitch, and the one most people use, is where the needle is held at an angle to the fabric: bring the needle up at A, back down at B, then up at C, working your way continuously along the line in this manner. Keep the spaces between stitches consistent, whether they are the same length as the stitches themselves, or a smaller measure.

BACKSTITCH

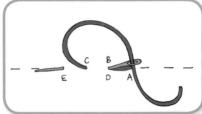

A great edging stitch; this is a running stitch variation – the difference here is that there are no gaps between the stitches. Bring your needle up through the fabric at A, take it back through the fabric at B, then along and up again at C. Take the needle back to B (D), and down through. Continue to work along the line in this way, ensuring your stitches are a consistent length. For added interest, you might want to weave a contrast colour through the finished row of stitching.

SEED STITCH

A great filler stitch that can be worked with single or double thread. For a convincingly random look, avoid parallel stitches and aim for each new stitch to be at roughly 45° to the last. As is the case for most running stitch variations, use a stabbing method if you want the stitches' appearance to be the same on both sides of the fabric

SATIN STITCH

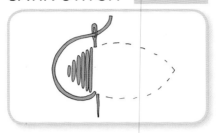

Satin stitch forms the basis of *Hardanger* embroidery, a style of whitework embroidery done on even-weave fabric. As well as being an excellent decorative and filler stitch, it is used to secure surrounding areas where warp or weft threads are to be cut and removed. It is also the perfect stitch to use if you want to completely cover a background, or fill in a shape.

Start by drawing your shape, then outline it with backstitch, as this will give you a clear boundary line to work to; skip this part of the step only if you are confident you can keep your stitches neat without it. Regardless of how neat a stitcher you are, if you are working on a fabric where it is difficult to count the threads, you will find it helps to stitch a boundary line anyway.

Bring the needle up on one side of the shape, then back down on the opposite side. Bring the needle back up alongside the start of your first stitch to start another. Repeat to fill the shape. Be careful not to pull threads too tightly or the fabric will buckle; then again don't let them sag or the background fabric will show through.

WOVEN RUNNING STITCH

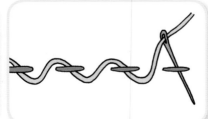

Once you have your row of running stitch, embellish it by weaving contrasting threads through the line of stitches. Push your needle in from the back of your fabric, where the running stitch starts, and zigzag your needle through the stitches.

SPLIT STITCH

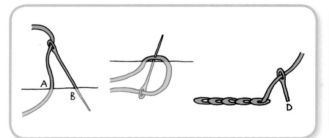

STEM STITCH

This stitch is similar to backstitch except you don't take your needle so far back, and you bring it up through the stitch you've just made. It is best worked with something like six-strand embroidery floss, as it's easier to split the stitch evenly.

Bring your needle up at A, and down at B. Take your needle halfway back along this stitch and bring it up at C, move along and take it down at D. Repeat as many times as needed. The stitches should be the same length on both sides of the work.

This is an excellent stitch for working curves! It is similar to split stitch except that instead of bringing the needle up through the stitch just completed, you bring it up alongside that stitch. So, bring the needle up at A, take it down at B, then up at C (halfway between A and B), then down at D, and so on until the line is complete.

COUCHING

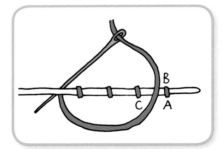

WHIP STITCH

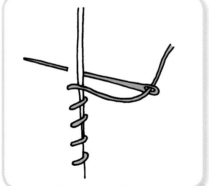

MENNONITE TACKS

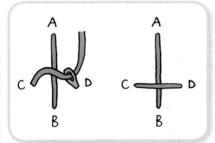

Couching is useful for securing found items to backgrounds, or for attaching threads that are too thick and unwieldy to pass through a fabric without damaging it. Use toning threads if you don't want the couching to show or use contrasting colours and make a feature of the couching stitches.

The method is simple: place the object (for example a piece of thick wire) on a background and temporarily hold it in place with a piece of tape to stop it sliding about. Bring the needle up at A, take it over the wire and back down at B (as close as possible to A). Bring the needle up at C, as close to the wire as you can; continue in this manner until the item is fully attached to background. Aim for tight little stitches that will prevent the couched object from sliding about within them.

Used in English paper piecing to join fabric folded over paper templates together, or for simply securing two fabrics, the aim is to make the stitches as discreet as possible!

Align the fabrics, then push the needle through the bottom layer of fabric. Bring the needle and thread over the top and back to the bottom layer of fabric in order to start the next stitch. The stitches will naturally slant to the right if you're right-handed, to the left if you're left-handed.

Make individual Mennonite tacks by bringing needle up at A, down at B, up at C, then down at D.

These can be worked in groups or randomly. If working in rows, create all the longest strokes first, then, using backstitch, work back along the row to create the cross bars. Continue until you have completed the row and knot off thread at the back of the work.

FLY STITCH

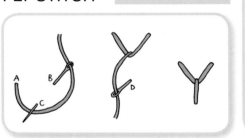

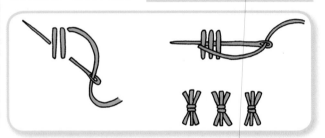

A fly stitch is an inverted 'V' or 'Y' (depending on how long you make the tail) that can be used randomly, or in ordered rows and columns. If working a column, it's an idea to draw guidelines on your fabric to help you maintain a consistent stitch width. To make a fly stitch, bring the needle up at A and down at B. Don't pull the thread too tightly but leave a little loop. Bring the needle up at C (the base of where you want your 'V' or the bowl of the 'Y' shape to be) and loop it over the stitch you made between points A and B. Now pull the thread to tension the 'V' or 'Y' shape. Take the needle back down at D to complete the stitch.

SHEAF STITCH

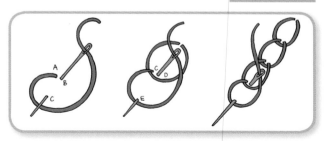

Start by making three parallel and equidistantly spaced straight stitches. The stitches can either all be the same height, or you could make the central stitch a little longer than the other two. Bring the needle up behind the central stitch. Slide the needle to the left and wrap all three stitches once or twice. Pull the thread to nip in the stitches and create the sheaf effect, then slide the needle to the back of the stitch and and knot off at the back of the work.

CROSS STITCH

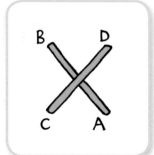

For perfectly neat and regulated stitches, Aida or even-weave fabrics will give the best results as many are designed specifically for cross stitchers. However, chicken scratch embroidery, which is worked on gingham, makes use of its checked pattern to produce equally pleasing cross stitch results.

SINGLE STITCHES
Bring the needle up at A, take it down at B, bring it back up at C and take it down at D. If the next stitch you want to work is not right nearby, tie off the thread at the back of the work rather than dragging it a long way – this can get messy and affect stitch tension.

GROUPS OF STITCHES
These are best worked in rows from left to right. Start by making a foundation row of right-leaning diagonal half cross stitches. Continue in this manner until the end of the row. Work back along the row from right to left to complete the crosses.

▶ LOOPED STITCHES

REGULAR CHAIN STITCH

There are several ways of working chain stitch, but the two types shown here are my preferred methods as I like to work towards, rather than away from myself. This is the method I learnt first.

Bring the needle up at A and back down at B. Do not pull the thread tight, but leave a loop. Bring the needle up at C so the needle is on top of the thread. Note that the distance C is from B determines the stitch length. Pull the thread tight to form the first link of the chain. Continue to make further loops in this way.

ISOLATED CHAIN STITCH

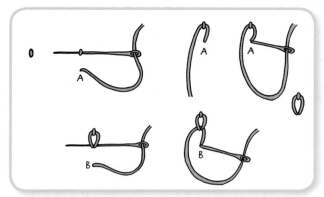

I learnt this technique more recently but it's increasingly becoming my favoured method as it helps me to produce stitches of consistent length. Start by making a tiny anchoring stitch, but don't pull the thread too tightly – you need to be able to slide your needle under it easily. Bring your needle up at A, which is a stitch length away from the initial anchoring stitch. Pass the tip of your needle through the anchoring stitch. Pull the thread to form a loop and anchor it by reinserting the needle at A. Bring the needle up at B, and slide it through the first chain stitch. Take the needle back down at B to form the next loop. Continue to work in this manner to form what is known as 'isolated chain stitch'.

LAZY DAISY STITCH

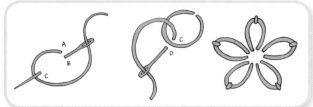

The lazy daisy stitch is really just five detached chain stitches arranged in a circle, where each loop is held in place with a tiny anchoring stitch. To help you space your petals evenly you might find it useful to draw a circle, divided into five equal sections onto a background fabric so you've got a guideline to work to. Start by bringing the needle up at A, and back down at B to form a loop. Do not pull the thread through, instead bring the needle up at C, over the loop and back down at D. Try to keep this stitch small and neat: it's the loop, or petal, that's the star of the show – not the anchoring stitch! When you've secured one loop, rotate the work by 72°, and bring the needle back up at A to start the next lazy daisy petal.

FEATHER STITCH

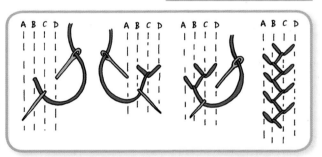

I like to think of this decorative stitch as a type of meandering fly stitch. It can look quite messy if you don't keep your stitches to an even width, so I suggest drawing guidelines to help you with spacing.

Bring your needle up on line B then down on line D, keeping the stitches at the same level. Bring the needle back up on line C – how far down the line you bring the needle back up determines the stitch length. Insert the needle on line A, to the left of, and parallel with where you brought it out at C. Turn the needle anti-clockwise and bring it up through the fabric on line B. Insert the needle on line D, (to the right of and parallel with where you brought it out at B) and bring it up at C. Continue in this manner, changing the direction of each new stitch as you work.

BLANKET STITCH

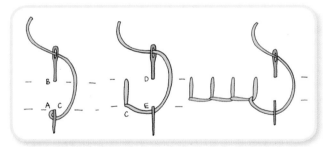

Perfect for binding edges, blanket stitch also works well as a decorative stitch. Try using it in wavy lines, or in concentric circles and closely packed rows to create an overall background texture. To make a basic blanket stitch, start by bringing the needle up at A. Take it down at B, and up again through the fabric at C, ensuring the thread is under the needle. To create the next stitch, bring the needle down at D and up at E. Continue to work thus until the work is complete.

BLANKET STITCH VARIATIONS

Why not vary the stitch length, combine long stitches with shorter stitches, or slant your stitches rather than have them standing straight to attention?

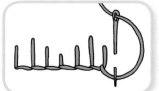

RAISED STITCHES

FRENCH KNOT

Everyone loves French knots – there's something so pleasing about them, especially when produced en masse. The only problem I find with French knots is that when using finer threads the knot doesn't always show, so I cheat, and either use my thread doubled up or, horror of horrors, wrap the thread around my needle more times than I'm supposed to!

Bring the needle up at A and wrap the thread twice around the needle's point. Insert the needle at B, which should be very close to A. Push the needle through the fabric while gently easing the knot off the needle. Aim for the knot to completely slide off the needle just as the eye passes through the fabric. Too soon before that and you may end up with an unwanted knot halfway down your thread. Pull the needle and excess thread through the knot and the fabric, then pull the thread to achieve a tight little knot.

BULLION KNOT

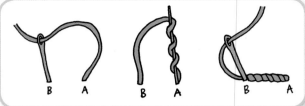

A bullion stitch is a bit like a travelling French knot; the principle is pretty much the same except when you reinsert your needle back into the fabric, after wrapping your thread around it, you do so a little distance away from where you first bought the needle out.

Bring the needle up at A then down at B, as if making a backstitch. Bring the needle up again at A but don't pull the needle all the way through the fabric. Instead, wrap the thread around the needle tip several times then slide the wraps along towards the fabric. Gently pull the needle through the wrapped threads, if need be holding them in place with your thumb to stop the wraps unravelling. Reinsert the needle at B to secure the stitch.

WHIPPED WHEEL

Whipped wheels are worked in a similar way to Dorset buttons (page 100) because you wrap, or whip, the thread around spokes to form textured ridges. You can create more texture and interest by padding the wheel, adding a bead to its centre, or using different coloured threads for the spokes and whipping stitches.

Start by making the spokes – uneven numbers look best – the stitches should have a common centre, and be evenly spaced or the finished wheel will look lop-sided. (Of course, you could make a feature of lop-sidedness and deliberately distort the distance between spokes!) You can make all of the spokes with long, straight stitches, or start them off with a fly stitch, then add more stitches to that.

Bring the needle up through the centre of the spokes, and take it under one of the stitches. Take it over the top, and back under that stitch, before moving on to the next spoke where you will do the same. As you work, be careful not to catch the background fabric, especially if you later want to pad the wheel. Continue to work in this manner, whipping the spokes, until they are all covered. It's important to keep an even tension and don't be tempted to cram too many rounds in as the stitches can get a bit lumpy which leads to a loss of thread definition.

WOVEN WHEEL

An alternative to the whipped wheel is the woven wheel. Create your spokes in exactly the same way as you would for a whipped wheel but instead of whipping each spoke, simply weave the needle and thread up and under alternate spokes.

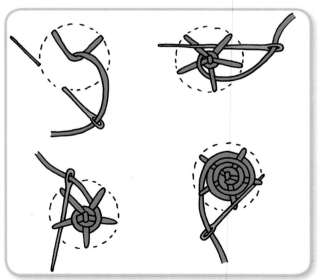

STITCH MIX AND MATCH

Most of the stitches used in this book are simply variations on a theme. For example, the dandelion and sycamore stitches here that I used in 'Stitched memories' on page 75 are a combination of chain and fly stitches that I've twisted to suit my needs.

SYCAMORE STITCH

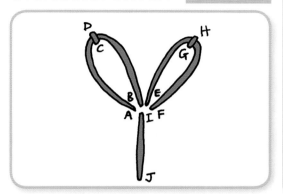

The sycamore stitch is simply two elongated lazy daisy stitches combined with a long straight stitch. Start by bringing the needle up at A, then back down at B to form a big loop. Secure it at points C and D with a tiny straight stitch. Create a second petal as you would with regular lazy daisy stitch but when you return to A, as if to start a third petal, simply finish off the stitch with one long stitch instead.

DANDELION STITCH

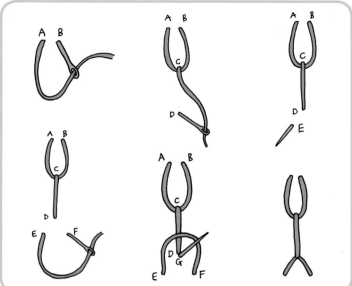

Here's how I made the dandelion stitch… Bring the needle up at A and down at B but leave the thread slack (as you would in chain stitch). Bring up the needle at C, hook it over the loop of thread, and down at D. Bring the needle up at E, then down at F to create another loop. Bring the needle back up at G/D, hook it over the loop, and pass it back down through the fabric at G/D to secure a tightened loop. Knot off the thread at the back of the work. In effect, I combined a skinny chain stitch with an elongated, upside-down fly stitch.

DRAWN AND PULLED THREADS

If, like me, you get a thrill out of pulling a piece of fabric to pieces and testing how many threads you can remove before it finally disintegrates, it's helpful to have at least a couple of *Hardanger* stitches in your repertoire. The most basic of these is overcast bars. Use them to bind an area where any central warp and weft threads are to be cut away. Or, use them to distort fabric tension and create the appearance of it having holes by tightly wrapping groups of weft or warp threads.

Decide on the number of strands you want to bind, and be consistent in always binding the same number of strands. Using something like an Aida fabric makes this much easier as strands are already counted into groups with prominent holes between them. Otherwise, use an even-weave fabric, which will have an equal number of warp and weft threads per square inch.

OVERCAST BARS

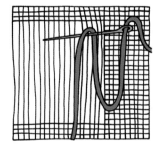

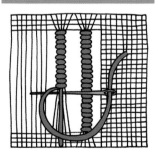

Leave a long tail of thread at the back of your work and bring your needle up through the centre of the number of threads to be bound. So, between strands 2 and 3 if binding 4 strands. Pass the needle over and under the strands, pulling them quite tightly to gather them in and create tension. Cover all the strands in this manner (concealing the long tail at the back of your work within the stitches) making sure that your stitches lie flat and don't overlap each other.

WOVEN BARS

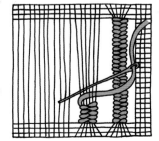

As with overcast bars, leave a long tail at the back of your work that you can cover with stitches as you go. Bring the needle up between the central strand of a group of strands, in this case between strands 3 and 4 of a group of 6. Take the needle over and under strands 1, 2 and 3. Bring the needle up between strands 3 and 4, then over and under strands 4, 5 and 6. Again, bring the needle up between strands 3 and 4; repeat until the threads are covered.

TEMPLATES

To enlarge or reduce the size of any template on the following pages use this simple formula: Desired size ÷ Original size × 100. This will give you the percentage, with which you need to increase or decrease the template.

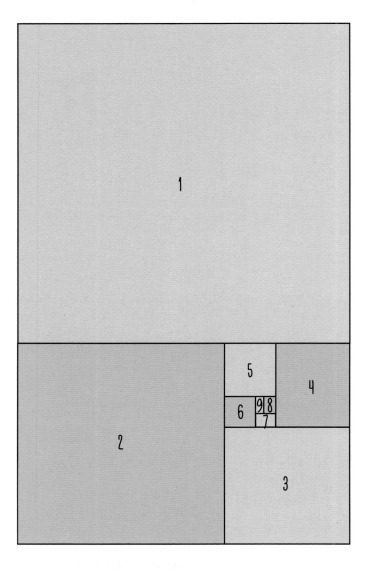

Pojagi patchwork

Given at 10% of actual size.

You can make this any size you like, but remember the larger you make your patchwork panel, the less fiddly the seams on the smaller pieces will be!

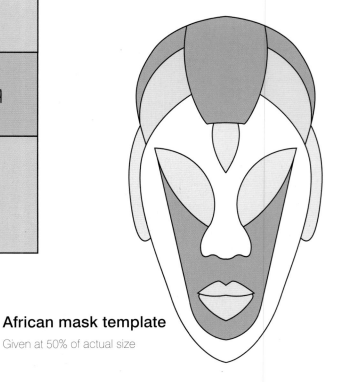

African mask template

Given at 50% of actual size

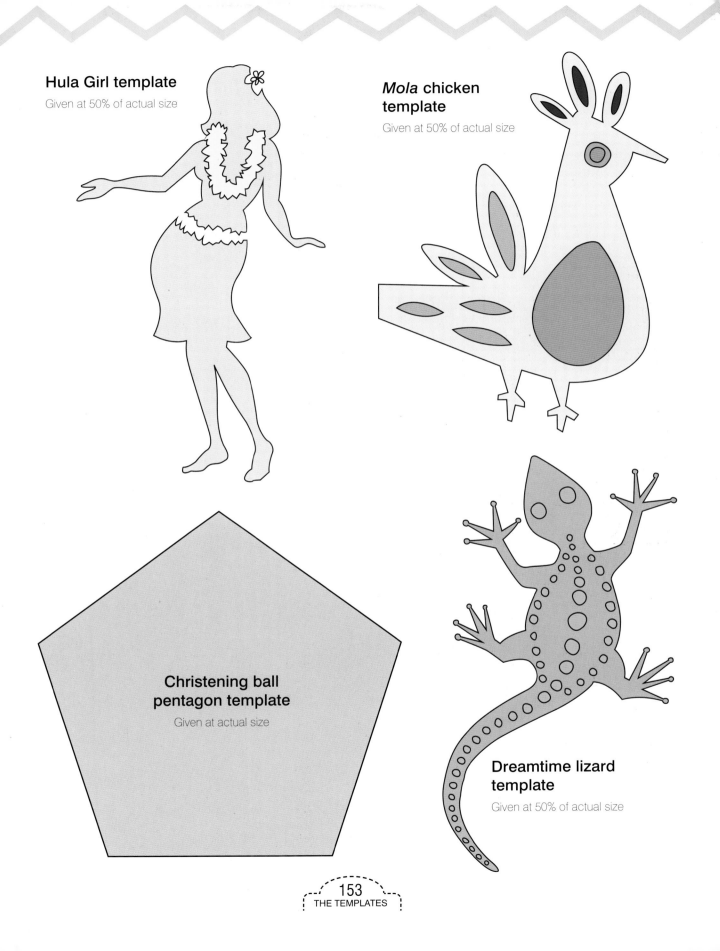

Hula Girl template
Given at 50% of actual size

Mola chicken template
Given at 50% of actual size

Christening ball pentagon template
Given at actual size

Dreamtime lizard template
Given at 50% of actual size

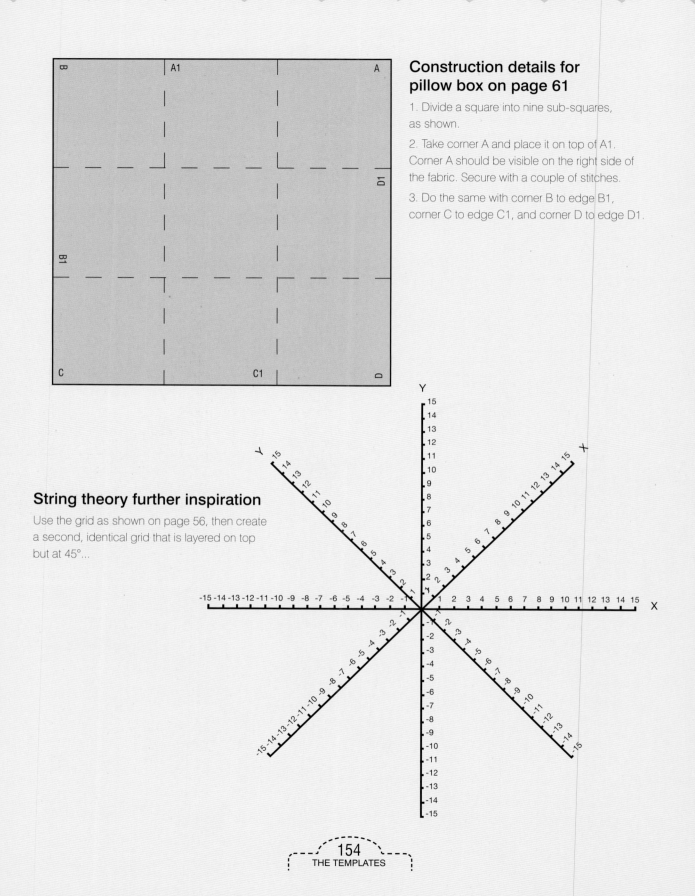

Construction details for pillow box on page 61

1. Divide a square into nine sub-squares, as shown.

2. Take corner A and place it on top of A1. Corner A should be visible on the right side of the fabric. Secure with a couple of stitches.

3. Do the same with corner B to edge B1, corner C to edge C1, and corner D to edge D1.

String theory further inspiration

Use the grid as shown on page 56, then create a second, identical grid that is layered on top but at 45°...

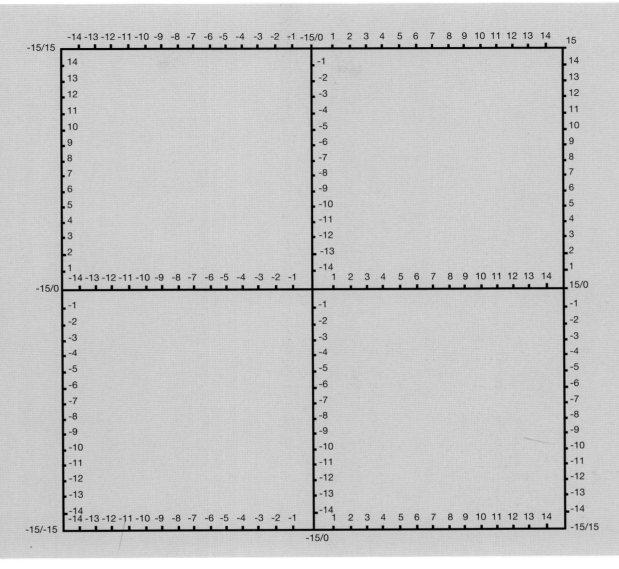

String theory further inspiration

Once you've built up your confidence, try this
more complex grid on for size...

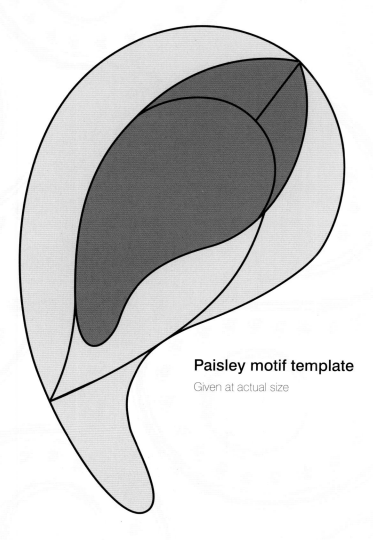

Paisley motif template

Given at actual size

In my example, which was created for a book with a height of 17cm ($6^2/_3$in), I created two vertical columns, each containing 17 holes. The rows were spaced 1cm ($\frac{1}{2}$in) apart, with each column 5mm ($\frac{1}{4}$in) apart. Adapt your layout to suit the size of the book you wish to make.

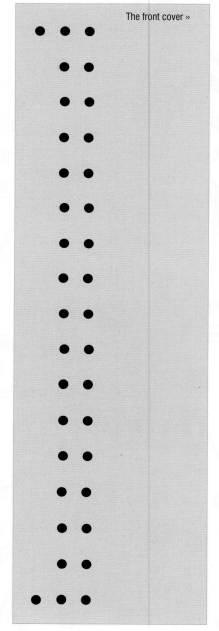

The front cover »

The spine of the book

A guide to Japanese bookbinding

There is no one correct way to do this: the number of holes in either the vertical or horizontal lines will contribute to the complexity of the design. I can, however, give you some general pointers when marking out and measuring:

• Make sure that your holes are not too close to the edge of the card, or they may not hold.

• For the pattern that I have given, ensure that you create an odd number of holes in each vertical line – you can increase or decrease the number, but it must be odd for the pattern to work.

• Keep the holes equidistant if you want to achieve the same finish as me – play around with the spacing if you want to experiment.

Fibonacci flower
template

Given at actual size

GLOSSARY

APPLIQUÉ a technique that involves stitching smaller pieces of fabric onto larger ones to make a pattern or design.

CREAM OF TARTAR an acidic by-product of wine fermentation used in natural dyeing to assist the mordant as it improves colour consistency.

CUBISM founded by Pablo Picasso and Georges Braque, Cubism took a revolutionary new approach to art, and how it represented reality. Multiple viewpoints of a subject would be depicted at once, leading to an abstracted, fragmented, yet fluid sense of form.

DADAISM a European *avant garde* art movement of the early 20th century. Much of the work was conceptual, and based on the rejection of bourgeois notions of 'good' art. Its most famous exponent was Marcel Duchamp.

DART a fold that comes to a point in order to shape fabric into a three-dimensional form.

DREAMTIME the mythology of the Australian Aborigines who believe the spirits of their sacred ancestors live in all things, from the ancient time of creation, on into the present.

ENGLISH PAPER PIECING a hand piecing technique where shapes of fabric are tacked/basted onto paper templates and then sewn together with whipstitch.

FREE MOTION EMBROIDERY a way of drawing with stitch onto a quilt sandwich, made possible by lowering the feed dogs (the grippy teeth that push the fabric along) and manually moving the fabric under the needle as you please.

FRENCH SEAM a seam with the raw edges enclosed.

FUSSY CUTTING where fabric is deliberately cut to focus on a specific element of a print such as a flower.

GÉLÉ a headdress or scarf worn by women in many parts of Southern and Western Africa.

HARDANGER a form of whitework done on even-weave cloth using counted thread and drawn thread work techniques.

MENNONITE TACKS resembling an elongated cross stitch, Mennonite tacks can often be found on utility quilts. The Mennonites were Christian groups belonging to the church communities of Anabaptist denominations named after Menno Simons (1496–1561) of Friesland in what is now the Netherlands.

MODERN QUILT MOVEMENT inspired by function and modern design, notable characteristics include bold colours and prints, high contrast and graphic areas of solid colour, improvisational piecing, minimalism, expansive negative space and alternate grid work.

MODERNISM a late 19th-/early 20th-century philosophical and artistic movement that broke with classical and traditional forms of design.

NEGATIVE SPACE the space in and around things that can be read in its own right, often forming an equally interesting shape as the main subject.

MORDANT a substance that combines with a dye or stain to fix it in a material.

OP ART aka OPTICAL ART this came to prominence in the 1960s. It uses optical illusions to give an impression of movement, pulsation, vibration or warping; hidden images may also be contained.

PAISLEY a distinctive motif of Indian origin resembling a curved teardrop.

RAG BOOKS for very small children made of strong cloth that cannot be torn.

REGISTER a method of correlating overlapping colours on one single image so the printed image doesn't seem to judder when viewed.

ROVING a long, narrow bundle of fibres produced during the process of making spun yarn from wool fleece, raw cotton or other fibres.

SELVEDGES the weft edges of a length of woven cloth. They are manufactured not to unravel and often carry the maker's information such as the name of the designer and the colour palette used.

SWISS DARNING here stitches are sewn on to garments to imitate knitted motifs and patterns. Can also be used to correct mistakes on colour work knitting such as Fair Isle designs.

TRAPUNTO a method of quilting whereby the underside of two layers of fabric is slit and padded, to produce a raised surface on the quilt.

UTILITY QUILT refers to a functional quilt containing a simple pattern and few frills. In the past, it was associated with the poor, or a 'make do and mend' approach, and might have included pre-worn fabrics such as work clothes, feed sacks and blankets.

WHOLE CLOTH where a single cloth (as manufactured) is used to produce a textile, such as a bedspread, rather than it being made from individually cut and combined pieces of fabric.

FURTHER READING

THOUGHT PROVOKING

Indigo: Egyptian Mummies to Blue Jeans
Jenny Balfour-Paul, British Museum Press

The Subversive Stitch: Embroidery and the Making of the Feminine
Rozsika Parker, I. B. Tauris & Co. Ltd.

Boro: Rags and Tatters from the Far North of Japan
Kyoichi Tsuzuki, Aspect Corp.

Selvedge Magazine
Published bi-monthly

INSPIRATIONAL

The Fabric of India
Rosemary Crill, V&A Publishing

The Quilts of Gee's Bend: Masterpieces from a Lost Place
William Arnett, Tinwood

Drawn to Stitch
Gwen Hedley, Batsford

Nancy Crow: Transitions
Nancy Crow, Breckling Press

Pauline Burbidge: v. 34 (Portfolio Collection)
J. Duffey Harding, Telos Art Publishing

Michael James: Art & Inspirations
Michael James, C & T Publishing

PRACTICAL

The Art of Manipulating Fabric
Colette Wolff, Krause Publications

50 Heirloom Buttons to Make
Nancy Nehring, Taunton Press Inc.

Pulled Thread Embroidery
Moyra McNeill, Dover Publications Inc.

Three-dimensional Embroidery Stitches
Pat Trott, Search Press Ltd.

Denyse Schmidt: Modern Quilts, Traditional Inspiration
Stewart, Tabori & Chang Inc.

The Stitch Bible: A Comprehensive Guide to 225 Embroidery Stitches and Techniques
Kate Haxell, David & Charles

The Stitches of Creative Embroidery
Jacqueline Enthoven, Schiffer Publishing Ltd.

Exploring Dimensional Quilt Art: Stitch, Fold, Embellish
C. June Barnes, Interweave Press

Quilt Artistry: Inspired Designs from the East
Yoshiko Jinzenji, Kodansha International Ltd.

The Ultimate Sashiko Sourcebook: Patterns, Projects and Inspirations
Susan Briscoe, David & Charles

Colour: A Workshop For Artists and Designers
David Hornung and Michael James, Laurence King

INDEX